'*Who Wrote Bacon* offers the _____ Shakespeare authorship question we have seen to date ... Ramsbotham's insight into these matters is precise, profound and indispensable. Without what he unveils in this book, we are simply left in the dark.'

Dr John O'Meara, author of *Othello's Sacrifice* and *Prospero's Powers*

'This highly exciting book opens up a new understanding of King James I and his connections to esoteric streams of his time. Furthermore, it gives valuable insight into the intriguing interrelationships between secret spiritual impulses and mainstream cultural life at the time of Shakespeare.'

Dr Kristin Rygg, senior lecturer at Hedmark University College, Norway; author of *Masqued Mysteries Unmasked*

'A book vital for English-speaking people and for our time.'

Terry M. Boardman, author of *Mapping the Millennium*

WHO WROTE BACON?

WHO WROTE BACON?

William Shakespeare, Francis Bacon and James I

A Mystery for the Twenty-first Century

Richard Ramsbotham

TEMPLE LODGE

Temple Lodge Publishing
Hillside House, The Square
Forest Row, RH18 5ES

www.templelodge.com

Published by Temple Lodge 2004

ISBN 1 902636 54 6

Cover by Andrew Morgan. Featuring: William Shakespeare, attributed to
John Taylor (detail), by courtesy of the National Portrait Gallery, London.
Francis Bacon, by Paul van Somer, c. 1618 (detail), from the Gorhambury
Collection, photograph by Photographic Survey, Courtauld Institute of Art.
James I, by Daniel Mytens, 1621, by courtesy of the National Portrait
Gallery, London.

Typeset by DP Photosetting, Aylesbury, Bucks.
Printed and bound by Cromwell Press Limited, Trowbridge, Wilts.

CONTENTS

ACKNOWLEDGEMENTS

I would like to express my thanks to the following:

To John O'Meara, for accompanying the book, his editorial ear, and for initially urging me to write it all down.

To Terry Boardman, for his wakeful accompaniment, and for urging me to publish what I had written.

To Sevak Gulbekian of Temple Lodge Publishing for midwifing and publishing the book.

To Francis and Elizabeth Edmunds, for lighting a fire and passing on a question.

To Alok Ulfat, for goads of encouragement and for his constant demand: 'freedom, responsibilty, *aesthetics*'.

To those at Park Attwood Clinic who first invited me to speak on Shakespeare.

To Andrew Wolpert, for requesting an article; to Andrew Wolpert and Sarah Kane for three evolving conferences at Emerson College on these themes, and to all their participants.

To the Humanities Section of the School of Spiritual Science for inviting me to speak on James I at two Summer Conferences (2002 & 2003). To all those participants who were open to what I shared, as well as those who were sceptical. They have been a spur.

To James de Candole, Rolf Speckner, Harald Hamre, Johannes Kiersch and a lady from Goerlitz for finding and sending me precious images and references.

To the late Gillian Dickinson, for a financial gift which has greatly helped towards this. I hope she approves.

To my parents, for help with a key image, and other generous assistance.

To Margaret Jonas and Francesca Josephson, ever-helpful, computer-free librarians, and to the staff of the British Library.

To Sally Parkes and Paul Schnellman, for their expertise and help with typing and with images.

To the worst a traditional English upbringing can inflict, for enabling me to perceive the problem.

To Elizabeth and Mary, who have watched over this book so patiently and so lovingly, from this side and from that.

'Tracking produces a kind of communion. Each clue draws you closer to the being that left it. With each discovery, your own tracks become more deeply entwined in the mystery you are following. Eventually, you absorb so many clues that the mystery and its answer are bound up inside you. The animal comes alive in your imagination. You can feel it moving, thinking, and feeling long before you come to the end of the string.

If you track fast enough, you eventually reach the end and find a set of prints with the animal's feet still in them.'

(Tom Brown Jnr: *Tom Brown's Field Guide to Nature Observation and Tracking*, Berkley Books, New York, 1983, p. 112.)

INTRODUCTION

The debate on the authorship of Shakespeare, far from slipping into the mists of irrelevance or being forgotten about through lack of interest, has perhaps never been stronger. The numbers of people who no longer believe that Shakespeare wrote Shakespeare has hugely increased, as has the variety of beliefs they hold as to who did. This year (2003), the first public conference of the Shakespearean Authorship Trust, chaired by Mark Rylance, was held at Shakespeare's Globe, with four main speakers defending the respective claims of William Shakespeare, Francis Bacon, the Earl of Oxford and Christopher Marlowe. John Michell's book *Who Wrote Shakespeare?*[1] has proved an extremely popular volume. This may well be because of Michell's generous and wide-ranging inclusiveness. Whereas small groups have previously staked out defensive claims for this or the other author, Michell, favouring none, reveals to our startled eyes the whole gamut of opinions. Michell even declares, towards the end of the book: 'The authorship question is so instructive and fascinating that it is a shame to limit it by prejudices, rather than enjoying the full range of its mysteries.'[2] He seems to be encouraging a new phase in the authorship debate—the sheer enjoyment of it, for its own sake, free of the need ever to reach clarity on the matter.

Michell himself is obviously not yet completely free of this need, for at the end of the book he suddenly surprises us by *almost* declaring himself in favour of Francis Bacon: 'If there was one mind and purpose behind Shakespeare, surely it was the subtle, devious mind and the practical, idealistic purpose of Francis Bacon.'

Michell acknowledges that there are clearly parts of Shakespeare that Bacon could not have written, but overcomes this problem by asserting that: 'The contributors to Shakespeare were drawn from various groups and coteries...' And only one person, in Michell's eyes, was capable of organizing such a project:

> At the centre of all plots and mysteries was Francis Bacon [...] only he could have dreamed up and set in motion a scheme for universal enlightenment, partly through the Shakespearian drama. Only he could have carried it through in such secrecy.

Even then, though, Michell can not quite leave it at that, and the final words of his book state that the riddle behind the authorship of Shakespeare remains, after all: 'A perfect mystery, dangerously addictive, but very worthwhile looking into.'[3]

I must confess that my own approach is very different from Michell's. It has, in the end, mattered very much to me to try and reach clarity on this question.

I first heard of the idea that Bacon wrote Shakespeare when I was about 11. I remember little more than registering it. I later read English at Cambridge, studying Shakespeare, though never specializing in him. As a lecturer in English literature at Warsaw University I even taught Shakespeare, once again without specializing. At no point during these 20-odd years was the question *Who wrote Shakespeare?* of any concern to me.

But in 1993 two events occurred which altered that dramatically.

One day, giving a class on W. B. Yeats, the absurdity of only ever speaking *about* literature was borne home to me. Literature needs to be performed and heard. If this does not happen, one is in exactly the same situation as if one only ever talked about Mozart, and never actually heard his music or, better still, performed it. I therefore gave up university work, returned to England, and did a four-year Speech and Drama training.

The other thing that happened was that I went to London one evening and saw an almost overwhelmingly powerful production of *Much Ado about Nothing*. It was the play's last night, and after the final curtain the main actor shared a few words with the audience. He began by thanking people, and above all: '...the spirit of Shakespeare, who was present'. However fanciful it may appear, this had also been my own exact impression during the evening. My disturbance may therefore be guessed at when I discovered from the programme that 'the spirit of Shakespeare', for this actor, almost certainly meant 'the spirit of Francis Bacon'. I was unable to get home afterwards, as my car had been clamped. I sat imprisoned in it in the dark, for several hours, which in retrospect seems fitting. To that single evening—and the questions it posed—I owe the 10 years of research that have led to this book.

My research took place in three main stages.

The first stage, focusing mainly on Shakespeare, led me to write an article called: 'In Search of William Shakespeare'. This was printed in *The Golden Blade, 1997*, under the editor's title: 'Shakespeare and World Destiny'. Parts of it are included, rewritten, in Chapter One of the present book.

Only after that had been written did a whole new vista to the subject open up for me. I had been aware of Rudolf Steiner's remarks about Shakespeare, many of which I had unearthed (for my article) from their hiding-places in various obscure journals, but there was one remark of his which, if I had heard, I had somehow closed my ears to, it not being what

I wanted to hear. Steiner states, unequivocally, that both Bacon and Shakespeare were *inspired* by the same individual, termed by Steiner an 'initiate'.[4] But he does not name this person. This statement gradually began to occupy more and more of my attention.

At about the same time I attended a lecture (by Sylvia Eckersley) on the authorship of Shakespeare. Afterwards, the writer and lecturer Terry Boardman asked if any connection could be seen between a particular historical individual and the works of Shakespeare. This small question triggered off a whole further period of research—into the history books, back into Shakespeare, and particularly into all that Rudolf Steiner had to say about this individual. One evening, dwelling on this material, it suddenly struck me, with a profound jolt, that it was *this* same historical individual who Steiner was seeing as the inspirer of both Shakespeare and Bacon. I researched this more and more, eventually felt able to lecture about it, and at a certain point found it necessary to write up the results of my research. These are to be found in Chapter Two.

Rudolf Steiner described his research as spiritual science—the *science* of the world of the spirit, which neither the senses nor the ordinary intellect can perceive. Steiner provides the methodology by which this world may nonetheless be perceived and known in ways which are equally, if not more, scientific than what is normally called sensible science—the science of the world of the senses. Whereas 'sensible science' depends on instruments with greater capacities of perception or calculation than our own, 'spiritual science'—or super-sensible science—depends on the development of our own inherent faculties of cognition.

Steiner did not set up a belief system, but instead encouraged people to develop the faculties that enable them to test what he says against their own experience. Nor did he consider it necessary for us to be clairvoyant before we start doing this. Our healthy powers of thinking, perception and judgement are enough for us to be able to test the truth or otherwise of his findings. Steiner makes an analogy with works of art—even when we lack the ability to *create* great works of art ourselves, we can still recognize and appreciate them, and even explore the truthfulness of all that is expressed within them.

As a result, many people have become able to place a certain trust in Steiner's research. This certainly involves living with the results of this research and continually testing them against one's own experience and judgement. But when, over many years even, they find this not to have been disappointed by Steiner, but instead to have borne consistently reliable fruit, just as with any great artist one has lived with over many years—Shakespeare, Mozart or Van Gogh—people develop a certain trust in this work, a certain immediacy of access to it, opening themselves more quickly than hitherto to receive what it may offer them.

For someone for whom this is the case, once they are certain of what Steiner is saying on the subject this book addresses, they may, I imagine, be fully prepared to grant it, in the first instance, the same kind of trusting acceptance they grant to his other work. The problem is, that regarding the question of Shakespearian authorship, in accord with the whole nature of the subject, it is very hard to know exactly what Steiner *is* saying. I hope that for some of those whose experience has led them to value Steiner's insights, my efforts to reach clarity on this, shared in Chapter Two, may prove helpful. It is in one sense written for them, as it is an extraordinary aspect of Steiner's research, of far-reaching importance, which has never yet been written about in English.[5]

If my research had ended there, in other words before Chapter Three, it might justifiably be said that what I have to say could only really hope to convince those who are able to trust the work of Rudolf Steiner. The book does not end there, however, and here I must make a confession.

Although I myself am someone who has come to appreciate the utter validity of Steiner's spiritual research, and therefore fully trusted what I realized Steiner was saying on this subject, I *never* expected the almost overwhelming abundance of supporting evidence and detail testifying to what he claims. As Steiner himself certainly did not arrive at his knowledge through studying all this material, I could even imagine that he would be surprised, and I hope delighted, to see his statements confirmed in this way.

I share what I have been able to discover in this regard— the third stage of my research—throughout the book, but mainly in Chapters Three, Six and Seven. The sheer abundance of this material also convinces me that I have only made a beginning in this area, which could, and I hope will be expanded by others with greater capacities and resources than my own.

This radically changes the book, in my opinion, from being a startling claim, of interest at best only to those with an openness to Steiner's work, to being a claim fully supported by all the relevant primary sources. The book is therefore intended to speak to anyone who has a sincere and open interest in the Shakespearian authorship question, or in the three individuals named in the book's subtitle. They will, I hope, be able to read Chapter Two as the book's hypothesis, and the remainder of the book as the grounding and supporting of that claim.

In Chapter Four I attempt to put all these discoveries into the context of some of the existing debate on the authorship of Shakespeare. In this regard, I have a rather difficult debt to acknowledge. The work of the Francis Bacon Research Trust has been the constant spur in relation to this work. Without it I would probably still sleepily be believing that Shakespeare wrote Shakespeare, and that was that. And yet what they have spurred me to is a position very different from their own. Chapter Four addresses the nature of this difference. Alongside my challenge to them, I hope they can also receive my gratitude.

All research, of course, involves combining what our thinking or our inner faculties provide, e.g. a hypothesis, with what is available to outer perception or research. In a question such as the inspiration behind Shakespeare, so clearly beyond the reach of our normal means of perception, though it is one to which many people now seek an answer, we need to rely to a far greater extent than usual on what our inner faculties can reveal. It is hardly surprising, therefore, that in order to answer such a question, we should have to attend to the remarks of someone like Rudolf Steiner, who developed great and trustworthy inner faculties. I could not myself have carried out Steiner's research, and this book is thus wholeheartedly indebted to him. I have then done what Rudolf Steiner did not do, namely ground his research in literary and historical detail, and set it in current context.

If readers can follow the details of what Steiner describes, and then of the supporting evidence, which provides such extraordinary confirmation of Steiner's claim, they will, I hope, concur that along this route we have indeed been able to uncover many of the mysteries surrounding the authorship of Shakespeare.

Chapter One

SHAKESPEARE THE ACTOR

Wherever people have questioned the identity of Shakespeare they have always agreed that there was an actor, called William Shakespeare, who grew up and died in Stratford-upon-Avon, and who must have acted in many of the plays that bear the name of Shakespeare. They say, however, that this actor, William Shakespeare, did not write the plays, but was merely a mask for the person or persons who did. There is almost always the assumption, furthermore, that a mere actor could not possibly have possessed what was necessary to write the plays of Shakespeare.

There is very little that needs saying if one wishes to defend the claim that Shakespeare the actor wrote Shakespeare's plays. One is not claiming that someone of far greater intelligence than Shakespeare wrote the plays, and therefore attempting to describe the lofty reaches of that intelligence. Nor is one claiming that someone far more important than a mere actor wrote the plays, and trying to elucidate the superior purposes of this individual. What one is claiming is that the plays were written primarily for the stage.

One's chief argument here is that there has never been another playwright who was so saturated in the dramatic medium, so completely a man of the theatre. For this reason Shakespeare's plays are second to none in their power, their life and their ability to affect an audience in performance. The people who can best affirm whether this is so are, in all likelihood, not academics, but actors and audiences.

Many academics, even when they are firmly of the opinion

that Shakespeare the actor wrote the plays, pay little or no attention to this. The audience-member's enjoyment and the actor's performance are of course hugely enhanced by ever-increasing insight, but only when this can be taken up by our artistic experience. In the end, the only thing to be done with a play by Shakespeare, as with a piece by Mozart, is either to perform or to hear it.

The very best book about the life of Shakespeare from this perspective has not surprisingly been written by an actor—*Shakespeare The Player, A Life in the Theatre*, by John Southworth.[1]

In his opening chapter, Southworth describes the gap in Shakespeare studies he is hoping to fill. For as long, he says, as the plays have been 'considered primarily as texts to be studied rather than as plays to be enjoyed, *Shakespeare the player and man of the theatre has remained in the shadows.*' (My emphasis.) He continues:

> While literally millions of words have been devoted to authorial and textual problems, few have thought it worthwhile or necessary to treat in any detail of Shakespeare's consecutive career as a player, or the possible ways in which his experience as an actor may have influenced his writing.[2]

Southworth suggests that the closing of the theatres in 1642, which, even when they re-opened in 1660, were never again to enjoy the life they had had in Shakespeare's time, is one of the major reasons for people losing a true sense of the whole context in which Shakespeare lived, acted and wrote. According to Southworth: 'Much that is now obscure and confusing in Shakespeare's life story is directly attributable to this break in tradition.' [3]

In his final chapter Southworth paints the picture of Shakespeare as someone who:

> ... abandoned a promising career as a narrative and lyric poet, aiming at publication, in order to [...] devot(e) all his energies to the *writing, production* and *performance* of plays for the looked-down upon public theatres of his day. For the three activities hung together, and I doubt he ever stopped to distinguish them in his mind, or to think of his acting career as separate from his writing career, or his writing and acting careers as separate from his responsibilities for their production and the 'instruction' of his fellows. He was not, as generally envisaged and presented by academic authors, a great dramatist who did some acting on the side [...] but a full-time, wholly committed, professional player and man of the theatre for whom the text of the play was not an end in itself (like any other book) but a means to an end—a performance on stage with himself as author, enabler and player. He was not a dramatist who became an actor for a time and, having made his pile, gave it up to enjoy rural retirement, [...] but an actor who became a dramatist, and never stopped performing, even after he had stopped writing plays, until fatal illness intervened.[4]

Harley Granville-Barker—another 'man of the theatre'—has perhaps, to date, been the most famous advocate of this approach:

> Can the full virtue of any art be enjoyed except in its own terms? [...] To transport Shakespeare from the world of the theatre into a vacuum of scholarship is a folly [...] The scholar, at best, will be in the case of a man reading the score of a symphony, humming the themes.[5]

The place where this viewpoint finds less well-known confirmation and support is in the work of Rudolf Steiner. The
gist of several brief references by Steiner to Shakespeare, in
lectures and essays at the turn of the 19th and 20th centuries,
may be stated as follows: the most important thing of all about
the plays of Shakespeare is *precisely* that they were written by
an actor.

As his remarks have seldom been quoted, I shall offer a
brief resumé of them. In 1898, in an essay entitled 'Another
Secret of Shakespeare's Works', Steiner set himself the goal of
discovering and defining Shakespeare's 'world view'. Having
described Goethe's 'world view', and that of several other
writers, he says that Shakespeare does not have a world view of
this kind at all. If he does have one, says Steiner, it could be
called 'the dramatic world view', for Shakespeare's approach
to every situation or character is always to seek out what is
most inherently 'dramatic' about them.

What Steiner is saying is that Shakespeare did not create
out of any *ideas* he had about his characters, or in order to
express a particular point of view, or world view, but created
out of the dramatic medium itself. Whatever is truly dramatic in a
situation or character—what will bring them to life most fully
on the stage—is the determining factor in Shakespeare's
plays.

Steiner reiterates this point in a lecture he gave in 1902:

> It is useless to ask what Shakespeare's own standpoint may
> have been on certain questions [...] Whether Shakespeare
> believed in ghosts and witches, whether he was a church-
> goer or freethinker, is not the essential point at all. He
> simply faced the problem: how should a ghost or a witch
> appear on the scene so as to produce a powerful effect
> upon the audience.[7]

He adds: 'The fact that this effect is undiminished today, proves that Shakespeare was able to solve this problem.' (!)

This essentially dramatic quality of Shakespeare's plays, Steiner tells us, is found in no other playwright in the same way, and is the reason for his continuing hold on people's imaginations today. Furthermore, it was a quality which, by definition, could only be achieved by someone with the most intimate and practical knowledge of the theatre and, primarily, of acting itself. It is no accident therefore that one can choose to overlook, but rather a necessity, discoverable from the plays themselves, that Shakespeare was an actor:

> Shakespeare's own works bear witness that he is their author. His plays reveal that they were written by a man who had a thorough knowledge of the theatre and the deepest understanding for theatrical effects [...] *In the whole literature of the world there are no plays which are so completely conceived from the standpoint of the actor.* This is a clear proof that Shakespeare, the *actor*, has the merit of having written these plays.[8] (My emphasis.)

***

There are different avenues by which we may approach what Steiner means by this striking statement that Shakespeare's plays are 'completely conceived from the standpoint of the actor'.

Firstly, there are all the central references in Shakespeare to drama and to acting:

> All the world's a stage
> And all the men and women merely players:
> They have their exits and their entrances;
> And one man in his time plays many parts. (*As You Like It*)

Life's but a walking shadow, a poor player
That struts and frets his hour upon the stage,
And then is heard no more. (*Macbeth*)

Often, of course, we, the audience, even witness this central, triple activity of Shakespeare's life—the creating,
rehearsing and performing of drama. In *A Midsummer Night's
Dream*, to our endless delight, we see not only the performance of the 'tedious brief scene of Pyramus and Thisbe' by
the 'rude mechanicals', but also a lengthy rehearsal of it. In
Hamlet we see Hamlet giving his famous advice to the actors
('Speak the speech . . . as I pronounced it to you, trippingly on
the tongue'), for the play he has partly written, and then the
performance itself of the 'play within the play', rightly seen as
one of the defining moments within Shakespeare. *The Tempest*
also has its play—or masque—within it, performed by Ariel
and his spirits, at Prospero's command. When it is over,
Prospero, the great theatre-magician, offers one last great
picture of the world as stage, with all its actor-inhabitants:

These our actors . . . / . . . were all spirits and
Are melted into air, into thin air;
And—like the baseless fabric of this vision . . .
The solemn temples, the great globe itself,
. . . shall dissolve,
And like this insubstantial pageant faded,
Leave not a rack behind.

The second way to observe the truth of Steiner's comment
is by looking at the way almost any individual scene of Shakespeare's *works* on the stage. If one is honest about this, one
can readily concur with Steiner that there are no plays more
thoroughly dramatic than Shakespeare's, down into every
detail. As any director or actor will tell you, every play, act,

scene and even speech of Shakespeare's is super-abundant in dramatic life. The plays work, on stage, in a way that no other plays have, before or since. The plays of Goethe, for example, however great a poetic and a scientific genius he may have been, are not a patch on Shakespeare's in this regard.

I am loath to give examples of this, as it is to be found in the whole of Shakespeare. As a tiny instance, however, we may think of the opening of *Richard III*. There is nothing remotely realistic about a character appearing, hunch-backed, and announcing: 'Since I cannot prove a lover ... I am determined to prove a villain ... Plots have I laid, inductions dangerous...' Untrue to life as this may be, however, it is utterly effective dramatically. Richard reveals himself to us in the very first speech of the play, and we alone, at that point, know of his true nature. The way Shakespeare unfolds a particular story is always determined by his consummate awareness of what works dramatically on stage. (One quickly learns to appreciate this aspect of Shakespeare by trying to write for the stage. Unless, like Bernard Shaw, one simply proclaims, quite undeservedly, one's own superiority, one soon recognizes Shakespeare's unrivalled mastery in this regard—in what might be called the ceaseless abundance of his dramatic imagination.)

The third way we can make sense of Steiner's remark is by contemplating the very thing which has so often caused such puzzlement about Shakespeare. His ability so completely to be *everyone* in his work, while appearing to be almost *no one* in his life.[9] This, of course, is precisely what the art of acting demands. It ceases therefore to be such a riddle, when we acknowledge the significance that Shakespeare was, after all, an actor. The point is well made by John Southworth:

If part of his peculiar genius as a dramatist and poet lay in his capacity to identify with the thoughts and feelings of his characters, and to speak with their voices out of the situations in which he had placed them, that authorial gift cannot have been wholly unconnected with the actor's ability [...] to identify with the characters he played [...] It is this protean component in Shakespeare's identity that leads so many biographers astray and confuses the critics.[10]

Giles Block is therefore wholly justified in saying (on the cover) of Southworth's book:

The emphasis on Shakespeare as player suddenly seems to be the element that has been missing in our search for a full and convincing portrait of 'the man Shakespeare'.

***

And yet...

There are also mysteries to what flows through Shakespeare which are not encompassed by this all-important fact of Shakespeare having been an actor.

This may account for his extraordinary dramatic genius, but not for the immense inspiration that flows through him. Where does *this* come from?

It is to this question we shall now turn, although we will first need to go by what may seem a very roundabout route.

Before we begin, though, I should add that, as Plate 1 is intended to show, it is by no means necessary, in seeking for the source of this inspiration to think that someone else literally *wrote* Shakespeare's work. The lion, it will be noticed, holds no pen.

Chapter Two

A RATHER TROUBLESOME PATRON

Rudolf Steiner's research

Whenever Rudolf Steiner spoke of James I he did so in a strange, enigmatic way, always pointing to greater mysteries than he could, at that present time, unfold. The first time he speaks of him, in March 1916, he does not mention him by name at all. In October 1918—in the first lecture of *From Symptom to Reality in Modern History*[1]—he discusses at some length a 'strange individual' who 'appeared on the stage of history' before eventually naming him as 'the historical personality of James I who reigned from 1603 to 1625'. In the following lecture he devotes four sides to speaking directly about James, but adds: 'It is not my task today—we can discuss this later—to speak of the many mysteries associated with the personality of James I.' It is not known what, if anything, was 'discussed later', but in the lecture itself Steiner tells us that although James was brought up as a Calvinist and had later converted to Anglicanism, 'in his heart of hearts he felt all this to be a masquerade which was foreign to him'. Nor, says Steiner, did any of James's contemporaries ever understand his point of view, as this seemed to be drowned out by all the other points of view jostling for attention: 'Nobody really understood what he wanted because all the others wanted something different.'[2]

James, born on 19 June (1566) under the two-sided sign of Gemini—the twins—has been described in history from startlingly opposite perspectives. After describing both of these, one highly positive and one extremely negative, Steiner comments: 'Those who characterized him from the one angle were mistaken, and those who characterized him from the other angle were equally mistaken.' As if this wasn't enough Steiner adds—most perplexingly of all, perhaps, in that James wrote several books—'...and the picture of him which we derive from his writings is also misleading. *For even what he himself wrote does not give us any clear insight into his soul.*' (My emphasis.)

James thus appears as a gigantic riddle, which not even what he himself said or wrote is able to solve for us. We stand before a veil, which only spiritual perception can penetrate: 'If we do not consider him from an esoteric point of view he remains a great enigma at the threshold of the seventeenth century.'[3]

In keeping with the mysterious nature of James we have already encountered, the slight lifting of this veil does not suddenly mean that all is 'explained', and unambiguously clear. Steiner seems to give us little glimpses, or fragments in various lectures, which it is up to us to try to piece together. Unlike his original listeners, we are at least in the position of being able to try to do so, as all his lectures, diligently transcribed, are now published. It is characteristic of Steiner's comments about James that nothing is straightforward, nothing ever too directly stated or clear. And there is *always* ambiguity. It is as if we meet again all the same riddles concerning this individual, but now transposed to the realm of the spiritual realities behind historical events and personalities.

The double nature of James, the seemingly completely contradictory ways in which he may be perceived, is nowhere more strikingly presented than in Rudolf Steiner's lectures *The Karma of Untruthfulness,* given in December 1916 and

January 1917. In Volume One Steiner calls James 'one of the most important occultists', and refers to him as 'James I who stands at the beginning of the renewal of the brotherhoods'.[4] In the context of all else that is being said here about these Western 'brotherhoods' and their interference in world politics, this is hardly to be seen as a complimentary reference, other than with regard to the sheer scale of the impulses which were working through him.[5]

The lectures translated as *Toward Imagination*,[6] given in 1916, elaborate on this sinister side of James I. Although Steiner now refers to him as an initiate, or as: 'James I of England in whom an extraordinary initiated soul lived', he is described by means of his complete contrast to the Jesuit philosopher Francisco Suarez: 'At the time of James I, a very ahrimanic[7] new development was inaugurated. Another development began with Suarez that was very luciferic.'[8] Thus, says Steiner: '...these two individuals, James and Francisco Suarez, are complete opposites'.

In Volume Two of *The Karma of Untruthfulness*, however, Rudolf Steiner speaks of James in completely different terms. Now we hear:

> One of the greatest, most gigantic spirits of the British realm stands quite close to the opposition against what is merely commercial within the British commercial empire, and that is James I. James I brings in a new element by continuously inoculating into the substance of the British people something that they will have forever, something that they must not lose if they are not to fall utterly into materialism.[9]

In Volume One, apart from the prime importance attached to commercialism by the brotherhoods, we also hear of their unambiguous intentions regarding the predominance of the Anglo-Saxon (we would now say Anglo-American) world:

> In the secret brotherhoods, especially those which grew so powerful from the time of James I onwards, it was taught as an obvious truth that the Anglo-Saxon race—as they put it—will have to be given dominance over the world in the fifth post-Atlantean period.[10]

This, says Steiner, primarily involves dominion by the English-speaking world over all peoples whose language is Latin-based. The brotherhoods, at the time 'when present events were being prepared', barely found it necessary to pay any attention at all to Central Europe, and the German-speaking world:

> In those secret brotherhoods little significance is attached to Central Europe, for they are clever enough to realize that Germany, for instance, owns only one thirty-third of the earth's land surface.[11]

This aspect, too, is directly contradicted by the way Steiner speaks of James I in the second volume of these lectures. For the 'new element' that James I 'inoculates into the substance of the British people' is, says Steiner: '...something that is linked by underground channels to the whole of the rest of European culture. Here we are confronted by a significant mystery.'

We certainly are!

In order to unravel this mystery a little, we must look more closely at the context in which this second, very different description of James appears. Rudolf Steiner has been speaking of the inner opposition that exists between the spiritual life of Central Europe and that of Britain. This opposition, he says, also sometimes takes the form of assimilating the other, and he gives the example of Shake-speare, who has been '...totally absorbed into German cul-ture. He is not merely translated, he is totally assimilated and lives in the spiritual life of the German nation.'[12] Thus: 'Standing in opposition can at the same time take the form of an absolute working together.'

As an example of this contrast between the cultures of Britain and Central Europe Steiner compares his own book *The Riddle of Man* with one by the British physicist and spir-itualist Sir Oliver Lodge: 'They are absolute opposites; it is impossible to conceive of any greater contrast.'

This constellation of diverging powers within Europe, says Steiner, only began after England and France had separated from each other, which Joan of Arc helped to achieve. Before that the whole of Europe, including England, had been to a great extent under the sway of what issued from Rome (either in the form of the Roman Empire, or the Holy Roman Empire of the Roman Catholic Church).

Referring directly to this 'differentiation between England and France', Steiner describes how everything then came about 'which was able to happen within the context of this differentiation'. And Steiner then tells us of 'the remarkable thing' that '*even from within this context*, the insight, the impulse springs up that a connection must be made with the opposite pole'. (My emphasis.)

What this leads to is the extraordinary phenomenon of 'the utterly British philosopher Francis Bacon of Verulam, the founder of modern materialistic thinking' being 'inspired from the same source as Shakespeare', who, in a manner quite opposite to Bacon, 'work[s] across so strongly into Central Europe'. And this is not the only link made from 'within this [western] context' with the 'opposite pole'—i.e. with Central Europe. For 'Jakob Boehme too was inspired from the same source. *He transforms the whole inspiration into the soul substance of Central Europe.* And again from the same source comes the Southern German Jesuit, Jakobus Baldus.' (My emphasis.)

Steiner beseeches us really to think through these differentiations, and not just vaguely jumble them all together; and then suddenly speaks of 'one of the greatest, most gigantic spirits of the British realm ... James I', which begins the quotation we are discussing.[13] Besides what we have already referred to, it gives a particularly striking picture of the nature of James's activity—described as 'pouring something into the substance of the British people—and doing so continuously and lastingly.'[14]

Let us summarize what Steiner is saying. The contrast is described between Britain and Central Europe. We are told that what is remarkable is that even *within* the western realm the impulse is born to create a link with the spiritual culture of Central Europe. This is achieved, we are told, through the fact that the same source that inspires the very British Bacon also inspires Shakespeare, who has such an affinity with Central European culture. This source also inspires Jakob Boehme, who transforms the same inspiration in a way suited to all that lives in Central Europe. It likewise inspires Jakob Balde. James I, says Steiner, one of the most gigantic spirits of the British realm, pours something into the substance of the British people, something that they must not lose if they are not to fall prey completely to commercialization, and something that links them very deeply with the whole of Central European culture. And he concludes by saying that 'Here we are confronted by a significant mystery.'

Seven years later, in April 1924, in his lectures on *Karmic Relationships*, Rudolf Steiner returns to this theme. Almost as a digression within a discussion of Francis Bacon, Steiner refers to 'the Bacon-Shakespeare controversy', where 'all manner of arguments are brought forward which are supposed to show that Shakespeare the actor did not really write his dramas, but that they were written by Bacon the philosopher and Lord Chancellor, and so on ...'

None of these arguments, says Steiner, 'get at the real truth'. And now he mentions once again the common inspiration behind Bacon, Shakespeare, Boehme and Balde, but this time is far more explicit about what he means by them sharing a common 'source':

> For the truth is that at the time when Bacon, Shakespeare, Jakob Boehme and a fourth were working on the earth, there was one initiate who really spoke through all four. Hence their kinship, for in reality it all goes back to one and the same source [...] Of course, these people who dispute and argue do not argue about the initiate who stood behind them, especially as this initiate—like many a modern initiate—is described to us in history as a rather intolerable fellow. But he was not merely so. No doubt he was so sometimes in his external actions, but he was not merely so. He was an individuality from whom went out immense forces, and to whom were really due Bacon's philosophic works, as well as Shakespeare's dramas and the works of Jakob Boehme, and also the works of the Jesuit, Jakob Balde.[15]

If we superimpose this paragraph on that of 7 years earlier, we realize, with what can only come as a profound shock, that it is James I who is described here—that James I is to be seen as the initiate standing behind both Bacon and Shakespeare. Where, in 1916, Steiner had directly mentioned James I, he now talks of an initiate 'described to us in history as a rather intolerable fellow'. When he mentioned James by name in

1916, Steiner had not yet made it clear that he was pointing to one initiate. In 1924, where this is clear, he chooses not to announce the name so directly.

When we put the two passages together, however, the truth becomes clear. A little less clear, perhaps, in English—for the original German for 'a rather intolerable fellow' is '*ein ziemlich lästiger Patron*'. Steiner's precise joke has completely vanished in translation. '*Lästiger Patron*' is a colloquial expression, which one might translate as 'intolerable fellow', but the literal meaning of 'Patron' is, of course, *patron*—James's exact earthly relationship to both Shakespeare and Bacon.

To make the matter clearer for ourselves, let us run through all of Steiner's few comments about King James in sequence.

Before we do so, however, we should remember another remark of Steiner's about King James. In 1916 Steiner describes how the development of both James and Francisco Suarez 'did not proceed in a straight line, but took place in a sudden jolt' through which they 'turned around, so to speak, and came from the unspiritual into the spiritual'. This kind of development 'can be compared to how we learn to read in elementary school—not by describing the shape of the letters, but by receiving an impulse through which we learn to understand the letters'. It is precisely in this way, and only in this way, I believe, that the 'significant mystery' of James I can be grasped. It will either leap into recognition for us, or it won't—it is not to be communicated by any too rigid spelling out of letters.

The very first time Rudolf Steiner spoke publicly about King James (28 March 1916) may be seen as a seed–description for everything else he said later. In the long first sentence, the description of James wraps around a description of Shakespeare:

> What is important is that at the beginning of the 17th Century, when Shakespeare had already created his plays which, in so far as they are History Plays deal in particular with the Wars of the Roses (the whole battle of the Red Rose and the White Rose is in fact to be found in Shakespeare's plays), that at the end of the 16th and the beginning of the 17th Century, a soul incarnated into a physical body in the realm of Britain, which did not work outwardly in such a significant way, but which worked with immense influence, over wide distances—over very wide distances spread an immense influence. This soul was able to work in a particularly stimulating way, which incarnated into a British body in which was mixed, in fact, not much British blood, but more French and Scottish blood. And from here something emanated that actually gave rise to the impulse both to external and to occult British cultural life.[17]

Only later on is James's name briefly mentioned in the lecture.

The next time Steiner speaks of James is in July 1916 in the lecture-cycle *Toward Imagination*. Having spoken in one lecture of the symptoms which point to what 'prevails these days', namely to the 'many occult movements in different societies', Steiner says:

> To a large extent the direction and attitude of modern thinking go back to the beginning of the fifth post-Atlantean epoch, when one spirit was setting the tone, and lived in the achievements of Bacon, Shakespeare and even of Jakob Boehme.[18]

In the following lecture he then mentions James I by name, and discusses him directly. Speaking once again of the 'occult movements' which 'prevail these days' Steiner points to their 'two main streams', which

> ...produce two typical, contrasting figures: James I of England, *in whom was living an initiated soul of a quite extraordinary kind,* and Francisco Suarez. The facts are clear, and when we connect them, we can answer one of the biggest questions of modern history.[19]

The 'combined influence' of these two streams, 'and particularly their fights against each other, shaped much of what lives and weaves in the present age'.

We next hear of James in the two lectures in *The Karma of Untruthfulness*—26 December 1916 and 15 January 1917. In the first of these, James's connection with the 'brotherhoods' is given once again. ('James I who stands at the beginning of the renewal of the brotherhoods.') In the second, which we have already discussed in detail above, the opposite, profoundly positive picture of James is added. With regard to the evolving sequence of these comments about James I, there is a significant difference between *Toward Imagination* (July 1916) and here (January 1917). In *Toward Imagination* Steiner spoke of the common inspiration behind Bacon, Shakespeare and Boehme in one lecture, and only a week later, in the next lecture, spoke of James I. Now, in January 1917, Bacon, Shakespeare, Boehme, Balde and James I are spoken of in the same paragraph.

In October 1918, in *From Symptom to Reality in Modern History,* just as on the very first occasion when he had spoken about James, Steiner discusses him at some length—referring to 'a personality who is especially characteristic of the emergence of the consciousness soul[20] in Western Europe'—

before eventually telling us his name. We have already quoted Steiner's statement that it was not his 'task' in these lectures 'to speak of the many mysteries associated with the personality of James I'. There is therefore no mention of the Bacon-Shakespeare mystery, as in the lectures of July 1916 and January 1917. However James *is* revealed as someone capable of combining the most radical opposites within himself. Having depicted 'two contradictory aspects of his character', Steiner comments: 'Whichever point of view we take, in both cases the cap fits perfectly.' Steiner also tells us, as we saw, not to seek in James's own work to learn about him: 'Even what he himself wrote gives us no clear insight into his soul'; and ends his extensive historical discussion by saying that if we *don't* look at the mysteries behind James, he will remain a closed book to us, a 'great enigma'.

In 1919 Steiner again mentioned King James in one of only two places where there is not some kind of riddle about the way James's name is mentioned. We shall discuss it in Chapter Five, as it does not relate directly to the Bacon-Shakespeare question.

From then on Steiner never again mentioned James I by name in a public lecture.[21] In 1920, however, he gave a lecture solely devoted to the Bacon-Shakespeare-Boehme-Balde question. It offers us a key to the whole riddle, and is, in fact, the crucial link between the two passages of 1917 and 1924.

First of all, we see Steiner making the all-important shift from saying that these four individuals were inspired from a common 'source', to saying they were inspired by the same 'initiate'. Steiner puts it as follows:

'The work of Bacon and the work of Shakespeare point to the same source—a source that is beyond the earth, *but which is represented in the earthly realm*.'[22] (My emphasis.)

A few lines later he elaborates on this:

From exactly the same source that the Bacon-Shakespeare inspiration stems from—*and even proceeding from the same initiated personality*—stem for Central Europe the spiritual stream of Jakob Boehme and of the Southern German Jacobus Baldus.

This unusual expression—an 'initiated personality' (*'Initiiertenpersönlichkeit'*)—echoes with Steiner's earlier statement about James I, that he had within him an 'initiated soul' (*'Initiierten-Seele'*).

The lecture is in many ways exactly the opposite of the one contained in the lectures on modern history. There the discussion was only about James I as a personality—or historical individual—and very specifically *not* about the 'many mysteries' connected with James I, such as the Bacon-Shakespeare mystery. Here, the discussion is only about that mystery and the historical personality of James I is never mentioned. What Steiner does give us though—in a kind of apologia at the beginning of the lecture for everything else he is about to say—is the whole basis of how we are to understand 'personality' in a connection such as this.

The lecture addresses directly all the resistance we are likely to feel on hearing that the initiate referred to is James I. As this resistance is still just as strong today I shall quote from it in some detail.

Having told us that we need to think very differently than we usually do about 'the influence of individual personalities in history', Steiner says:

It is usually imagined that a great man in history—be he distinguished in art, in statesmanship, in religion, or however—works through the impulses that he himself consciously brings to expression; it is generally assumed that this is the sole channel of his influence. And one then goes on to consider his activity, and to ask: What did he do? What did he say? What kind of relation did he have to other men? And so on.

As a matter of fact, when we are considering persons of outstanding significance in the evolution of history, the thing is not so simple. His real influence upon the evolution of mankind depends on *driving spiritual forces*, which are active behind history and which come from the spiritual world. Personalities are in a sense no more than the channel through which these driving spiritual forces are able to work into and influence the course of earthly history.

This does not preclude the fact that there is at the same time a considerable admixture of individual subjectivity in the influence of such leading personalities. Obviously that is generally the case. But we shall only acquire a right idea of history when we recognize that whenever a so-called great man speaks, the leading spiritual powers in human evolution are speaking through him, that he is, as it were, merely the symptom of the presence of certain driving spiritual forces. He is the door through which these forces find entry into the course of history.

We are not to be put off then by a historical individual's personality, but should focus instead on the spiritual impulses working through him. Steiner reiterates:

And so when we cite some leading personality of a particular period in history and try to characterize his influence upon the whole configuration of his age, this does not imply—if we are speaking from the perspective of spiritual science—that we want to lead you to believe that this man's influence was to be traced entirely to the force of his personality.

The influence of such a leading individual cannot be confined only to those people who directly encounter his work:

> ...for the person in question [. . .] is only the expression of forces which stand behind him, and the wider circles of mankind are also being influenced and impressed by these same forces. In this personality one only sees what is working in the age.

One might ask, in the light of the last sentence, what the actual achievement is of such an individual. Steiner clarifies this in words which may also help us to understand how a spiritual stream can be 'represented in the earthly world':

> Some spiritual stream, some spiritual tendency might be working in a particular direction, perhaps quite subconsciously, among wide circles of human souls. And the presence of this spiritual stream might come to expression in one single person in such a way that what the rest only dimly divine, what wide circles of people, perhaps whole peoples, dimly divine, he formulates in clear ideas.

When we remember that Steiner said of King James that 'even what he himself wrote does not gives us any clear insight into his soul', the words that follow also become particularly pertinent: 'This person might never commit his ideas to writing and perhaps never even speak of them at all.'[23]

Of course, says Steiner, 'the very opposite is also quite possible, that a personality may exercise a widespread influence among the people of his age'. But, in this particular lecture, 'it was necessary to put the other side quite clearly and explicitly, to prevent misunderstanding'.

I find it possible to imagine that Steiner was quite prepared in this lecture to name James as the initiate behind Bacon and Shakespeare (and Boehme and Balde), and that it shows us all the efforts Steiner needed to make in order to prevent the misunderstandings that could arise, and the resistance people would be likely to feel, should he do so.

One further possible misunderstanding is that if the initiate referred to is King James, this might seem to infer that this impulse, which also deeply permeated Central European culture, through the works of Jakob Boehme, is to be seen primarily as a 'British' impulse:

> Someone might say [. . .] that when we describe a person as having significance for a particular epoch, we are giving a description of something that is happening in one small corner of the world, whereas the real interest lies in hearing a description of what is taking place among the wide masses of mankind. As you will see, the thing is not to be taken in that way at all.

It is only once all these misunderstandings are out of the way that Steiner begins the main part of his lecture.

The rest of the lecture gives us further insight into the whole Bacon-Shakespeare (and Boehme-Balde) question, particularly regarding the relationship it reveals between the cultural life and spirituality of central Europe and Britain. Such is the significance of this that at the end of the lecture Steiner directly counters any suggestion that the matters he is discussing are 'remote from everyday life':

> The questions upon which I have here touched lie in reality at the foundation of the urgent world problems that face us today. We shall never be able to find an answer to the great question as to the true relation between East and West, between Europe, Asia and America, unless we go right back to the things of which we have spoken today.[22]

The two crucial points this lecture raises—that one 'initiated personality' stood behind the four, and that we must not let ourselves be put off by what we know of the earthly 'personality' of leading individuals—are picked up and taken even further in 1924, in Steiner's last and most complete treatment of this theme. Knowing all this background our ears should now be far more sensitized to Steiner's words than when we merely hear them out of context.

Going even further than the phrase 'initiated personality' he now speaks directly of 'an initiate' ('*ein Eingeweihter*'):

> The truth is that at the time when Bacon, Shakespeare, Jacob Boehme and a fourth were working on the earth, there was one initiate who really spoke through all four. Hence their kinship, for in reality it all goes back to one and the same source.

And now he is able to relate what he said about the potential hindrance to us of our knowledge of someone's earthly personality to the historical individual who *was* this initiate:

> Of course, these people who dispute and argue [about the authorship question] do not argue about the initiate in the background, especially as this initiate—like many a modern initiate—is depicted in history as a rather troublesome patron.

Steiner could not have been any clearer on the matter than this. He goes on:

> But he was not merely so. No doubt he was so sometimes in his external actions, but he was not merely so. He was an individuality from whom immense forces proceeded, and to whom were really due Bacon's philosophic works as well as Shakespeare's dramas and the

works of Jacob Boehme, and also the works of the Jesuit, Jacob Balde.

We also know of a few private conversations Rudolf Steiner had on this theme. The last of these was a mere three days before he died, with Albert Steffen.[24]

Content-wise we learn little more than that Steiner spoke of his research into 'Shakespeare, Jacob Balde, Boehme and Bacon' and 'pointed to their common source of inspiration'.

Steiner had first spoken directly on the issue of Bacon and Shakespeare in 1900, when he said: 'I am today not yet in a position to form a judgement on this great question.' Thus Steiner's concern with the question lasted from at least 1900 until the very end of his life. Knowing how ill Steiner was, one cannot help being struck by Steffen's experience of the conversation: 'While he was speaking, so forcefully and full of joy, it was possible to believe that his crisis would be overcome.'

The most extraordinary thing of all, though, about this conversation, is its date—27 March 1925—300 years, to the day, after the death of James I.[26]

I hope I have, by this point, said enough for the shock of recognition to have happened for at least some readers. As I said earlier, the thing cannot be proved in a normal way, but can only 'leap across the wires' to us. Once this has happened, however, and we then read the whole sequence of Steiner's remarks, it is no longer possible for us to be in any doubt which historical figure Steiner is referring to.

Why so riddling?

What we must still ask, though, is *why* Rudolf Steiner speaks in this strange, riddling manner about James. I am aware of no

other person about whom he speaks in a way so veiled in
mysteries. Nothing is ever straightforward. Everything is gone
around and hinted at, so that it never seems possible to clearly
take hold of what is said. In all but two of the places[27] where
James is mentioned there is some kind of riddle about the *way*
his name is mentioned. Why? It cannot just be that in
speaking about James—particularly when connecting him to
Shakespeare and Bacon—Steiner was trying to out-English
the English in diffuseness of expression.

Looking back over all we have discovered, we can now see
two clear reasons for this. Firstly, as we have discussed, James's
spiritual development 'did not proceed in a straight line, but
took place in a sudden jolt'. Steiner compared the way this jolt
worked to 'how we learn to read in elementary school: not by
describing the shape of the letters, but by receiving an
impulse through which we learn to understand the letters'.

It would be a spiritual untruth for Steiner to speak in a way
that did not accord with this. He therefore cannot spell out
the secrets of James's nature letter by letter. All he can do is
to place the relevant letters next to each other, and in the
right sequence. From then on, something will either leap
between them for us, enabling us to read them, or it won't.
There is no other way for this mystery to be conveyed. This
also, I may add, tells us quite a lot about how James's
inspiration may have worked 'over great distances' ('*weit,
weithin*') upon Bacon and Shakespeare, as well as upon
Boehme and Balde. This should not be thought of as happening in too spelled-out a manner, but more by way of an
impulse which they received.

The second reason has to do with the whole riddling
question of whether what we are talking of is to be ascribed to
the *personality* of King James. The only answer we can give to
this question is: it is and it isn't. Hence Steiner's strange 'now

you see him, now you don't' depiction of James, where repeatedly he both is and isn't named.

The reason for Steiner describing this mystery in the way he did is not because he intended us permanently to remain in doubt about it. When Steiner says: 'Of course [...] people [...] do not argue about the initiate in the background', he clearly expects us to become able to do so. Steiner spoke about this mystery as he did because we need to understand it in the right way. The riddle is not to do with whether King James is to be seen as the initiate behind Bacon and Shakespeare, but only with *how* he is to be seen as this initiate.

A question of Christian Rosenkreutz

We are, of course, in a far more fortunate position here than Rudolf Steiner's original listeners. We are able, unlike them, to put side by side everything he had to say on this subject, without which the leap is very hard to make. When we do so it takes, in my opinion, almost wilful obstinacy not to let the thing leap into recognition for us.

Understandably, therefore, it never seems to have occurred to early anthroposophists[28] that the individual Steiner was referring to could have been King James I. It somehow came to be assumed that the initiate must have been Christian Rosenkreutz, and this was then passed on almost as received wisdom. Several early anthroposophists, to whom we are greatly indebted, not least for their research into Shakespeare, King James I and Rosicrucianism, declared publicly that Steiner was referring to Christian Rosenkreutz. Isabel Wyatt and Margaret Bennell say so, as do Karl König, Ernst Lehrs and Francis Edmunds.[29] It is not without trepidation that I contradict such esteemed company. As so many others have also believed this to be the case, or believe it today, it is necessary to briefly address this issue directly.

Steiner tells us that the reason people who have noticed a kinship between Shakespeare and Bacon never discuss the initiate behind both of them is that 'this initiate—like many a modern initiate—is described to us in history as a rather intolerable fellow'. Christian Rosenkreutz is not 'described to us in history' at all. The historian Frances Yates has researched in great detail the Rosicrucian movement at this time, and no outer evidence she discovered led her to believe in an actual individual named Christian Rosenkreutz. I have been asked if Steiner was perhaps referring to the Comte de St Germain, in whom Steiner tells us Christian Rosenkreutz was reincarnated.[30] But Steiner's words leave no ambiguity: '*At the time* when Bacon, Shakespeare [...] were working, there was an initiate there ...'[31] (my emphasis). This cannot possibly have been the Comte de St Germain, who was not even born at the time.[32] Nor can it in any way be said that because Christian Rosenkreutz is such a difficult, unlikely figure, we have a problem in thinking of him as this initiate. We very much *like* to think of this initiate as Christian Rosenkreutz, whereas we experience exactly the kind of resistance Steiner describes when asked to think that he was James I.

Nowhere does Steiner mention Christian Rosenkreutz in the vicinity of these remarks about Bacon, Shakespeare, Boehme and Balde. Nor when Steiner does speak of Christian Rosenkreutz is there any mention of this mystery. It is speculation, therefore, to start thinking of Christian Rosenkreutz at this point. We find, by contrast, that there is a whole series of gradually developing comments about James I and these other four individuals, and that these all culminate in the remark about the 'troublesome patron'.

People have believed that if we are to consider the

individual who stood behind Shakespeare, Bacon and Boehme (we know less about Balde)[33] then Christian Rosenkreutz must surely be the only individual of a stature great enough to achieve this. But I venture to state that, immense—'gigantic'—as the one must be whom Steiner refers to in this context, the tasks of Christian Rosenkreutz are greater still. Difficult as it may be to talk of limits in describing such immensities, Steiner *only* speaks of the work of four individuals being inspired by this initiate, whereas the influence of Christian Rosenkreutz cannot, I believe, be confined in this way. It seems completely unfitting to circumscribe the activity of Christian Rosenkreutz to the particular task of standing directly behind these four individuals.

This is *not* to say that there was no Rosicrucian influence on James, and therefore also on Shakespeare, Bacon,[34] Boehme and Balde. An initiate of the time would obviously, one imagines, be open to such influence. But I suggest that too great a claim has been made about the 'special relationship' of Shakespeare, Bacon and Boehme[35] to Christian Rosenkreutz. Rudolf Steiner states that because of the initiate standing behind him, Francis Bacon must be seen in the philosophic realm as 'the instigator of an immense and far-reaching stream of time'. These are almost exactly the same words Steiner used about James I,[36] which makes sense when one sees James as the initiate.

If we see the initiate as Christian Rosenkreutz then we are saying that the work of Francis Bacon and the work of Christian Rosenkreutz are, in like manner, *the same.* This viewpoint is by no means only held by people who express indebtedness to Steiner's work. Peter Dawkins, for example, states this in *Francis Bacon, Herald of the New Age.*[37] 'Francis Bacon [...] was the true Fra. Christian Rose Cross, the "Father" of the Rosicrucian Fraternity which announced its existence in the early 17th Century.' This obviously ignores the existence of an initiate behind Bacon, and of the individuality named Christian Rosenkreutz, but if we see Bacon's works as 'really due' to Christian Rosenkreutz then we cannot, I believe, quibble too much with Dawkins's picture, or with his statement regarding the supposed discovery of Christian Rosenkreutz' tomb in 1604: 'The "tomb" is analogous to Bacon's Pyramid of Philosophy.'

This is, on the one hand, to claim too much for Francis Bacon, and on the other to belittle the true spirituality and influence of Christian Rosenkreutz.

A question of James I

If instead we see James I as the initiate behind Bacon, we gain a somewhat different picture. It was James I, says Steiner, who 'gave the impulse for both the exoteric and the esoteric [occult] cultural life of Britain'.[17] James, he says, 'stands at the beginning of the renewal of the brotherhoods'.[38] It was the spiritual influence of James, 'one of the most important occultists', which underlay the choice of his son-in-law Frederick, the Elector Palatine, as King of Bohemia.[38]

If we look not only at what has been written by those aware of the work of Rudolf Steiner, but also at the literature currently—and popularly—emerging from Britain about the spiritual origins of British cultural life, we find that much of it does indeed say of Francis Bacon almost exactly what Steiner says of James. Bacon is seen as the great inspiring figure, or initiate, behind British cultural life. He is seen as the founder of Freemasonry. Most of this literature also places great emphasis on the whole movement allied with Frederick, Elector Palatine, and its intimate connection with British cultural and spiritual life through Frederick's marriage in 1613 to Elizabeth, daughter of James I. Francis Bacon himself wrote a Masque, which was performed at the wedding celebrations.[39]

Rudolf Steiner, of course, is by no means wholly positive in his discussion of all this, and of the influence of these 'brotherhoods', unlike much of the current British literature.[40] That at present, however, is not my point. My point is that everything this literature describes as the occult activity of Francis Bacon matches exactly what Steiner says about King James, which makes sense when we see James as the initiate behind Bacon. It does not match what Steiner said about Christian Rosenkreutz.

Of course, the literature about Bacon does not speak of any initiate behind Bacon, and certainly not of James I. James I has on the whole received a standardized picture as someone opposed to all things occult. (This is possibly because James would not ally himself with the spiritual movement that found such a focus in Frederick and Elizabeth, in which Bacon is seen as so influential.) This movement has, in much of the present literature, come to be seen as synonymous with Rosicrucianism,[41] as if there was no more to Rosicrucianism than this. But as more emerges about this time, this view of James is becoming increasingly difficult to maintain. People have been puzzled by such things as the Rosicrucian Christmas greeting sent to King James by Michael Maier (see Plate 17), and Robert Fludd's dedication of *Utriusque Cosmi Historia* to King James.[42] Adrian Gilbert expresses further puzzlement over the fact that: 'For all his dislike of occultism, James I is the first British monarch definitely recorded as having been a Freemason.'[43]

The outer details—or some of them—of James's connection with Freemasonry have only recently begun to emerge.

These have been most extensively documented by Robert Lomas in *The Invisible College*, subtitled *The Royal Society, Free-masonry and the Birth of Modern Science*. Lomas's researches about this previously unexplained side of King James lead him to re-question the nature of the connection between King James and Francis Bacon. Lomas's questions, arising from examination of the outer evidence alone, are of immense interest when set against Rudolf Steiner's picture of Francis Bacon, and of the 'rather troublesome patron' who inspired him. Lomas asks:

> Was it just coincidence that [Bacon's] first serious attempt to develop notions on how science should be approached, occurred in the second year of the reign of James VI (I)? Bacon had not addressed the question of how to study the mysteries of nature before James arrived from Scotland. Did he learn of some new philosophy from the court of James VI (I)?

Lomas briefly sums up his chapter on this theme as follows:

> Francis Bacon had never been a particularly good scientist but in the later third of his life he took an interest in techniques for studying nature. It was, however, only after the arrival in England of King James VI(I) that this interest in science developed. [...] Bacon is depicted on the fron-tispiece of Thomas Spratt's *History of the Royal Society* amidst a welter of Masonic symbolism. Bacon also made great use of Masonic symbolism in his own writings and on the covers of his books. Again, his use of Masonic symbolism only began after the arrival of King James in London. [...] I decided I needed to look more closely at [...] King James VI (I).[44]

Chapter Three

TRACES IN BACON AND SHAKESPEARE

Bacon

When we do look more closely at Bacon's link to James I we cannot but be surprised at what we discover.

The Advancement of Learning, the book Lomas refers to as having been published in 'the second year of the reign of James I', 1605, is written almost in the form of a conversation with King James. Each of its two parts is not only nominally addressed 'To the King' but begins with a lengthy preface in praise of James, the argument of which extends into the main text, which continually re-addresses itself to 'your Majesty'.

The praises of King James in the prefaces are of no common order. They lead eventually to Bacon comparing King James with Hermes Trismegistos:

There is met in your Majesty a rare conjunction, as well of divine and sacred literature, as of profane and human; so as your Majesty standeth invested of that triplicity, which in great veneration was ascribed to the ancient Hermes; the power and fortune of a king, the knowledge and illumination of a priest, and the learning and universality of a philosopher.[1]

We should be wary of seeing this merely as expedient flattery of the King, particularly as Bacon expressly denies this:

Neither am I moved with certain courtly decencies, which esteem it flattery to praise in presence. No, it is flattery to praise in absence; that is, when either the virtue is absent, or the occasion is absent; and so the praise is not natural, but forced.[2]

And again:

> *I am well assured that this which I shall say is no amplification at all, but a positive and measured truth;* which is, that there hath not been since Christ's time any king or temporal monarch, which hath been so learned in all literature and erudition, divine and human.[3] (My emphasis.)

Bacon's *Novum Organum (The New Organon)* is also dedicated and prefaced to King James: 'This Regeneration and Renewal of the sciences is rightly due to the times of the wisest and most learned of all Kings.'

As he had in *The Advancement of Learning*, Bacon compares James to King Solomon:

> You rival Solomon in so many things, in gravity of judgement, in the peace of your kingdom, in the largeness of your heart, and finally in the remarkable variety of books which you have composed.[4]

It was in these terms that Bacon asked James to provide the necessary support for his own scientific endeavours, encouraging James to 'emulate that same King in another way, by taking steps to ensure that a Natural and Experimental History be built up and completed'.

This enables us to see that King Solamona, in Bacon's *New Atlantis,* is also to be equated with King James.[5] This king is specifically connected, as his name suggests, with the Biblical King Solomon, 'finding himself to symbolize in many things that King of the Hebrews'. The highest point of this connection is the kinship between Solomon's 'Natural History' and Solamona's similar achievement, his setting up of the institution named 'Solomon's House' dedicated to the study of the 'Works and Creatures of God'.[6]

Bacon's *Henry VII* also has strong links with King James. One editor of Bacon's works writes that Bacon, after his impeachment, asked the King: '...to direct his mind to any undertaking that might add lustre to his reign. The history of Henry VII was pointed out by the monarch as a work worthy of his pen.'[7] I have not found the exact letters Devey was referring to, but Bacon certainly sent James a copy of the book in manuscript, saying:

> I durst not have presumed to intreat your Majesty to look over the book and correct it, or at least to signify what you would have amended. But since you are pleased to send for the book, I will hope for it.[8]

And earlier the same year, Bacon, on trial for receiving bribes, made the King the following strange offer:

> Because he that hath taken bribes is apt to give bribes, I will go further and present your Majesty with a bribe. For if your Majesty give me peace and leisure, and God give me life, I will present your Majesty with a good History of England, and a better digest of your laws.[9]

In a letter to King James regarding *The New Organon* Bacon states that even though his scientific method only allows what can be experienced by the senses, whatever King James might have to say will be included as an exception (!):

> For though this work, as by position and principle, doth disclaim to be tried by anything but by experience, and the resultants of experience in a true way; yet the sharpness and profoundness of your Majesty's judgement ought to be an exception to this general rule.[10]

As Lisa Jardine rightly comments, therefore, *The New Organon* must be seen as: 'a collaborative undertaking between the Sovereign and his Lord Chancellor'.[11]

What we discover, in fact, on examining the connections of Bacon's works with King James, is that, far from being a matter of a few random, flattering remarks, there is a consistent thread running through Bacon's major works—*The Advancement of Learning, The New Organon, The New Atlantis* and *Henry VII*. It is not enough to say that the majority of Bacon's work is dedicated to King James. External evidence even shows it to be the result, in a sense, of *collaboration* with James.

Finally, Bacon makes a number of comments about his relationship to King James which describe, better than anyone else could do, what we have been referring to:

> I have ever been your man, and counted myself but an usufructuary of myself, the property being yours.[12]

> This work is but a new body of clay, whereinto your Majesty by your countenance and your protection, may breathe life.[13]

> As I have often said to your Majesty, I was towards you but as a bucket and a cistern; to draw forth and conserve; whereas yourself was the fountain.[14]

Shakespeare

If we find evidence of this kind in the case of Francis Bacon, one might ask whether anything similar is also visible with William Shakespeare. We gradually discover that this is indeed the case. It is a question primarily, of course, of seeing in what way the influence of King James can be discerned in

Shakespeare's work after 1603, when James came to the English throne. We will look first of all at three plays where this influence is most incontrovertible.

In 1603 itself Shakespeare seems to have paused, completing, unusually, no play in that year. On 26 December 1604, *Measure for Measure* was performed in the banqueting hall at Whitehall, before King James and others. Much has been written about the similarities between Vincentio, the enigmatic Duke in the play, the 'fantastical duke of dark corners'[15] and James I. The Arden Shakespeare concludes its three-page discussion of this by saying:

> To see the Duke [...] as an exact replica of James would be to misunderstand both Shakespeare's dramatic methods and the practice of the contemporary stage. But to suppose that no parallel was to be drawn between the two characters, or that, according to the familiar formula, 'any resemblance to any living person was purely accidental', would seem to be just as untenable.[16]

Macbeth, first performed in 1606, may almost be seen as a template for the kind of collaboration we are considering between Shakespeare and his patron King James. Often termed 'The King's Play', though people generally are not aware which King is meant, it has also been called 'King James's Play'[17] and 'The Royal Play of Macbeth'.[18] Those who have studied the background of *Macbeth* are well aware of the intimate connection of the play with King James. James had his own intense encounter with witches and witchcraft in 1590, after returning from Denmark with his bride Queen Anne of Denmark. Witches were said to have attempted to conjure up storms, so that the ship bearing the royal couple would never reach Scotland. The elaborate details of this, together with the King's personal appearance at the trials of the witches, where he ordered them to perform part of their ritual in front of him, continue to make gripping, if at times highly disturbing reading.[19] James is directly referred to in *Macbeth* as a descendant of Banquo, and therefore as the true inheritor of the throne of Scotland, as well as in connection with the divine right granted to the throne of England.[20] James is in this sense saluted by the play as the first ruler of the joint thrones of England and Scotland—of 'Great Britain'. Attention has also been drawn to the influence to be found in *Macbeth* from 'the strong theological bias of James's mind'.[21] Almost wherever one looks in *Macbeth*, it seems, evidence of King James may be found.

It is not my intention to explore this in any detail, but merely to indicate that the closeness of Shakespeare and James is particularly visible in *Macbeth*. Thus Ted Hughes, who is certainly not interested in seeing the play from a simplistically historical perspective, comments: 'There cannot be much doubt that Shakespeare shaped his play under an arc-light awareness that this Scot was his principal audience.[22] John Wain goes even further, reminding us of what Lisa Jardine had to say on the interaction between James and Bacon:

> Shakespeare's imagination was enormously receptive. When James ascended the throne, a great many English people read his works from natural curiosity, and Shakespeare would hardly have been less curious than they [...] *Macbeth* is beyond doubt the result of this saturation. So that we might say that *King James and the greatest of his subjects* [Shakespeare] *were, for this occasion, collaborators.*[23] (My emphasis.)

The third play where the influence of James on Shakespeare is undeniable is *Cymbeline*. In *Shakespeare's Last Plays*, Frances Yates devotes a whole chapter to the symbolic connection of the character of Cymbeline with King James. She alludes to both Cymbeline and James having two sons and a daughter, and relates the hugely important role within the play of Cymbeline's son-in-law, Posthumus Leonatus, to James's son-in-law, Frederick, Elector Palatine. At the end of the play, according to Yates, 'All is to be healed in a new imperial peace, a new outpouring of the divine in the holy reign of Cymbeline–Augustus–James.'

Clear evidence of the identity of Cymbeline and James is found when we compare *Cymbeline* and a passage from Shakespeare's last play, *Henry VIII.* At the end of *Henry VIII* (subtitled '*All is True*'), bringing history right up to Shakespeare's own day, Archbishop Cranmer prophesies that the monarch—James I—who succeeds Queen Elizabeth:

> . . .from the sacred ashes of her honour
> Shall star-like rise, as great in fame as she was . . .
> And, like a mountain cedar, reach his branches
> To all the plains about him. (Act V, Sc. V, l. 54.)

Cymbeline also contains a prophecy regarding the future destiny of Britain, and the 'cedar' in the prophecy is specifically related (by the 'soothsayer', Philarmonus) to Cymbeline:

> The lofty cedar, royal Cymbeline,
> Personates thee. (Act V, Sc, V, l. 154.)

So intricate, in fact, is the whole political level of *Cymbeline*, with reference to Great Britain, that it has drawn fruitful comparison with Ben Jonson's Court Masques, which often depended for their meaning on the actual presence of King James, around whom the events of the Masques revolved, and before whom they were enacted. Thus Leah Marcus writes:

If we immerse ourselves in the Jacobean materials to which
Cymbeline seems persistently to allude, we will discover that
the play, like a Jonsonian court entertainment, is far more
deeply and persuasively topical than even its most avid
political 'lock-pickers' have found it to be.[24]

Although this is what we expect to find in a Masque, we certainly do not normally expect it in Shakespeare, which is
perhaps why even now several scholars are unsure of exactly
how to place *Cymbeline* within the whole of Shakespeare's
oeuvre. It is almost as if in *Cymbeline* a geological layer breaks
through to the surface and becomes visible, which in other
plays remains hidden. What this layer shows, as it did in
Macbeth, is a quite remarkable commonness of purpose
between Shakespeare and his royal patron, King James.

In these three plays—*Measure for Measure, Macbeth* and
Cymbeline—the relationship between Shakespeare and King
James is at its most visible. Yet exploring a little further we
discover, to our amazement, that some kind of link between
Shakespeare and King James has been detected in every single play of Shakespeare's from 1603 onwards. Once again, I
shall not discuss this in detail but only point to it. In the only
sustained treatment there has been of the outer connections
between Shakespeare and King James, *Shakespeare, the King's
Playwright,*[25] Alvin Kernan examines these links closely in
seven plays: *Hamlet,*[26] *Measure for Measure, Macbeth, King Lear,
Antony and Cleopatra, Coriolanus* and *The Tempest,* and mentions them in several others. Kernan sums up at one point:

Whatever King James may have written as a young man in
his *Short Treatise* about the necessity for poets avoiding
matters of state, year after year his official playwright
offered the King and his court not mere entertainment but
plays dealing obliquely and tactfully, but nonetheless

palpably, with the issues that most seriously engaged the court: the law (*Measure for Measure*), primogeniture and witchcraft (*Macbeth*), kingship (*King Lear*), court corruption (*Antony and Cleopatra*), unrestrained generosity (*Timon of Athens*), the crisis of a martial aristocracy being transformed to a court noblesse (*Coriolanus*), empire and the uses of art (*The Tempest*).

Apart from *Cymbeline* and *Henry VIII*, which we have referred to already, this only omits three of the twelve plays Shakespeare wrote during James I's reign—*Othello, Pericles* and *The Winter's Tale.* In *Shakespeare, The Jacobean Plays*, Philip McGuire points out how in *The Winter's Tale* and *The Tempest,* both performed at the festivities for the marriage of James I's daughter Elizabeth to the Elector Palatine in 1613: 'The son of one ruler and the daughter of another become betrothed, establishing the prospect of uniting through their offspring the states their fathers rule separately.'[27]

We might also note that one of these sons, Florizel, in *The Winter's Tale*, is heir to Bohemia. Eight years after the play was written, in 1619, Frederick was to become King of Bohemia. In the following paragraph McGuire also relates *Pericles* to King James: 'James's life also offers evidence of a pattern of events like the one particularly prominent in *Pericles* and *The Winter's Tale*; a ruler's eventual triumph over extreme and sustained adversity.'

Regarding *Othello*, the first of Shakespeare's plays to be performed before King James (1 Nov 1604), McGuire points out:

The Turkish threat to Cyprus in *Othello* is one of the background events leading up to the battle about which King James had written a poem, *Lepanto*, published in 1591 and again on his accession to the throne of England in 1603.[28]

Kernan detects a verbal parallel, conscious or not, between King James's description of:

A bloodie battel bolde...
Which fought was in Lepantoe's gulfe
Betwixt the baptiz'd race
And circumcised Turband Turkes.

and Shakespeare's 'circumcised dogs' and 'malignant and turbaned Turks' (*Othello*).[29] Elsewhere Kernan describes Othello in a way remarkably fitting to the double nature of King James we have described—though Kernan presumably did not intend it this way. Othello's strange fate, says Kernan, is to end up: '...as both the Turk and the destroyer of the Turk, the infidel and the defender of the Faith'.[30]

I am fully aware that for the most part these comments merely point to *external* connections between King James and the work of Shakespeare. I am not claiming that they provide evidence for all I have been saying about James's influence on Shakespeare; nor, heaven forbid, am I suddenly advocating a purely political interpretation of Shakespeare's plays.[31] What they show, however, exactly as we have seen with Bacon, is that the connections with King James in Shakespeare's work, far from being occasional or random, are maintained consistently and profoundly through everything Shakespeare wrote from 1603 until his death.

What we have described in Chapter Two about the inspiration of Shakespeare requires us to consider an *inner* influence from King James, not merely an external one. Jane Jack comes closest to this when she speaks of *Macbeth* being influenced by the 'strong theological bias of James's mind'.[21]

If we accept such an inner influence it would mean that the extraordinary unfolding journey of Shakespeare's plays, described for example by Ted Hughes, might also be seen as a reflection of James's inner development. *Measure for Measure, Macbeth, King Lear, The Tempest*—to name but the most out-standing—could then also be seen as huge and profound stages of James I's inner growth. This is something that I believe could eventually be attempted; it would involve bringing together the outwardly observable links with King James (e.g. in *Macbeth*) with the inner drama of the plays.

Kernan's book—*Shakespeare, the King's Playwright*—attempts no such thing. He gives us an immensely detailed description of all the interrelationships between Shakespeare and King James, while completely ignoring the possibility of any inner influence. He reminds one in the end of someone who has chanced upon Aladdin's lamp, sensed there to be something hugely important about it, and therefore described for people in every detail its exact shape, size and physical char-acteristics, without discovering the one thing that makes it so important—the genie inside!

We shall return to this theme in Chapter Six and Seven, and also look at the biographical connections that can be found between Shakespeare and King James.

Chapter Four

WHO WROTE BACON?

Our researches have brought us deep into the terrain of the 'authorship debate' on Shakespeare. Let us recap, for a moment, what we have discovered. The first chapter attempted to show how Shakespeare, the actor, is to be seen as the author of his own plays, their superabundant life being due precisely to Shakespeare's unequalled mastery of the world of the stage and the dramatic medium. We quoted Rudolf Steiner's statement, for example, that: 'In the whole literature of the world there are no plays which are so completely conceived from the standpoint of the actor.' If we think of Shakespeare, however, in the full fire of his creativity, writing 37 plays in 18 years, in the midst of a hectic life as both actor and theatre-manager, it is not hard for us to see that Shakespeare was *inspired*, was on the receiving end of an immense inflow of inspiration, from which our culture has been so deeply nourished over the last 400 years. Heminges and Condell, Shakespeare's friends, and the editors of the First Folio, testify to the seemingly effortless way in which Shakespeare received inspiration: 'His mind and hand went together, and what he thought he uttered with that easiness that we have scarce received from him a blot in his papers.'[1]

It is admittedly a further step, which we attempted in Chapter Two, to seek the source of that inspiration.

It is only Rudolf Steiner, to my knowledge, who has professed to be able to speak on this with any certainty, from his own powers of 'exact clairvoyance' or 'spiritual science'. He presented this as the rightful extension of scientific activity from the realm of the natural world, where it has until now focused its attention, to non-sense-perceptible, spiritual realms of existence. During Steiner's lifetime (1861–1925) his extension of science in this direction was pioneering to the most radical degree, whereas today, almost exactly 100 years after his first pronouncements on spiritual science,[2] the climate is very different, and we witness a considerable resurgence of interest in spiritual realities. The *context* Steiner spoke in was different from ours, and this can make his work appear inaccessible; but if we make the effort to grasp what he is saying, the sheer detail of his spiritual-scientific research, besides its depth and extraordinary scope, show that it still has unparalleled insights to offer.

Rudolf Steiner describes Shakespeare as being inspired from a source in the spiritual world, and states that Francis Bacon was inspired from exactly the same source. We may also speak of a 'who' however, for this source was 'represented in the earthly realm' by an initiate, who 'stood behind' both Shakespeare and Bacon. This initiate 'spoke through' both Shakespeare and Bacon, and it was therefore to him that 'were really due Bacon's philosophic works, as well as Shakespeare's dramas'.[3]

The identity of this initiate has, of course, only been discussed by people aware of this statement by Rudolf Steiner. These have, with one notable exception,[4] presumed that Steiner was referring to Christian Rosenkreutz. By looking at the exact wording of Steiner's comment, and by comparing it with many other comments on the same theme, we have discovered something different. As long as we do not allow ourselves to be side-tracked by thoughts of his personality, and can see him instead as the representative of a source or stream within the spiritual world, we may see that the individual referred to is, in fact, James I.

The authorship debate revisited

This is what Rudolf Steiner's research reveals in relation to the whole question of: 'Who wrote Shakespeare?' which might therefore, with equal justice, be phrased: 'Who wrote Bacon?'[4] It has been discussed before in German,[4] but never to my knowledge in English. As England is the original home of the whole Shakespeare–Bacon debate it is important that we try to set these discoveries within the current context of this debate.

My own first major encounter with the 'Bacon-Shakespeare controversy' was at a workshop on *Measure for Measure* in 1993 organized by the Francis Bacon Research Trust, with Peter Dawkins and Mark Rylance. I continue to be grateful for that encounter, and British cultural life as a whole has huge reason to be grateful to Mark Rylance, both as a performer, and as artistic director of Shakespeare's Globe. Over the last ten years, however, I have come to a standpoint different from that of Peter Dawkins. By describing what that difference is I shall attempt to put into context what I have been saying. This is by no means an easy matter, as we shall discover that there is far more at stake than merely a quirky discussion about the authorship of some of the world's greatest plays.

Peter Dawkins, and there are many others of the same opinion,[5] is firmly convinced that, to put it simply, Bacon wrote Shakespeare. This is to put it *very* simply, for Dawkins sees Francis Bacon as 'avataric':

There is a very great deal that is misunderstood or not generally known about Francis Bacon and the colossal work that he put into operation, including the fact that he was one of the world's great mystics, as well as being a cabalist, and one of the finest poets the world has ever seen.

Working with the Mystery traditions, what this great master set in motion is quite remarkable and unique. His incarnation and his work had been foreseen and prepared for by others for many ages prior to the event, and is avataric in scope.[6]

This is to say, at the very least, what Steiner said of Bacon, that we must see in him (in the philosophic realm) 'the instigator of an immense and far-reaching stream of time'.[7]

What is remarkable in what Dawkins is saying, if we compare it with what we have described, is first of all that he—and others who think like him—has very definitely seen the inner kinship of Bacon and Shakespeare, which most people are quite unaware of. Rudolf Steiner sees this inner kinship as the result of their being inspired by the same initiate, which Dawkins does not address, but in seeing the unity behind Bacon and Shakespeare he clearly has a powerful sense, as others do not, of the presence of this initiate.

The genuine perception that Dawkins has of the workings of this initiate is one reason, I believe, for the increasing influence of what he says and writes about Bacon and Shakespeare. He perceives an immense spiritual stream running through them both, which undoubtedly exists, which people are increasingly open to, and which satisfies a genuine spiritual thirst.

To an extraordinary degree Dawkins sees through the works of Bacon and of Shakespeare to the spirituality of this initiate; but, I believe, mistakenly sees Francis Bacon himself as this initiate. It is remarkable how much of what Dawkins and other 'Baconians' say about Bacon tallies exactly with what Steiner says about the initiate in the background, whom we have identified as James I. To this initiate, says Steiner, are 'really due' the plays of Shakespeare and the writings of

Bacon. This is what Dawkins says about Bacon. Bacon is also credited by 'Baconians' with responsibility for the King James Bible. Thus Edwin D Lawrence, author of *Bacon's Shakespeare*, wrote:

> The 1611 Bible is without possibility of doubt, one of Bacon's books. [...] When Bacon was born, English as a literary language did not exist, but once he died he had succeeded in making the English language the noblest vehicle of thought ever possessed by mankind. This he accomplished merely by his Bible and his Shakespeare.[8]

Needless to say, if we see King James as the initiate behind Bacon and Shakespeare we can credit him with his own Bible! Thirdly, we remember Rudolf Steiner saying that James I 'stands at the beginning of the renewal of the brotherhoods' and that to James can be traced back Britain's contemporary cultural life, both in its external and its occult forms, among which Steiner certainly includes the Freemasonic brotherhoods. This colossal founding influence in the sphere of Freemasonry is something that Dawkins and many others also ascribe to Francis Bacon, calling him: 'the founder and first Grand Master of Modern Freemasonry'.[9]

On this last point, as we have pointed out, researchers have recently—almost only since the beginning of the 21st Century—begun to become aware of the primary role of James I in the inauguration of modern Freemasonry. Thus Adrian Gilbert writes: 'It would seem to be James I [...] who was responsible for bringing Freemasonry to England.'[10] Robert Lomas also observed that Bacon's Freemasonry only began after King James's arrival in London in 1603, and was profoundly influenced by James's presence. However, if we are prepared to replace Dawkins's picture of Francis Bacon with Steiner's picture of the initiate behind both Bacon and

Shakespeare, then in these three instances of Shakespeare, the King James Bible and the founding of Freemasonry, we are in a good deal of agreement about the substance of the claims that are made.

The matter is very different, though, with some of Dawkins's other claims about Francis Bacon. We have had reason to refer to the Rosicrucian movement, and to its founder Christian Rosenkreutz. In 1604, at the time of Shakespeare, Bacon and James I, *The Chymical Wedding of Christian Rosenkreutz* was written, which described in mysterious terms the initiation of this individual in 1459, clearly to be seen as the central event of his life, which ended in 1484. We know this date from the *Confessio Fraternitatis* (1615), one of the two Rosicrucian manifestos, which also describe other events in Christian Rosenkreutz's life. Rudolf Steiner also spoke from many different angles about the life, initiation and continued influence of Christian Rosenkreutz. It is not our intention here to attempt to paraphrase or explore these descriptions, other than to point to their extensive and detailed nature.[11]

One thing Rudolf Steiner does make clear is how Christian Rosenkreutz works behind the scenes of human history, only in the rarest of instances appearing on the stage of outer events.[12] Rudolf Steiner, from his own spiritual-scientific research, gives us careful and intimate descriptions of the working of this individuality, both with regard to events in the 15th Century, described in the Rosicrucian documents of the 17th Century, and with regard to his activity in the 17th Century itself.

Frances Yates finds no outer evidence for the existence of Christian Rosenkreutz, which is not surprising in view of what Rudolf Steiner has said. Because of this lack of evidence, Frances Yates doubts there ever was a *real* Christian Rosenkreutz. This points perhaps to the limitations of a history almost only *allowed* to discuss what is substantiated by tangible documentary evidence. Peter Dawkins, however, declares that Christian Rosenkreutz was, in actual fact, none other than Francis Bacon: 'Francis Bacon [. . .] was the true Fra. Christian Rose Cross, the 'Father' of the Rosicrucian fraternity which announced its existence publicly in the early 17th Century.'[13]

Many other people have now begun to share this thought, for example Adrian Gilbert in *The New Jerusalem*: 'The stream of thought that Baconism represented in England was not merely sympathetic to Continental Rosicrucianism, in many ways it was identical with it.'[14] But this statement of Gilbert's[15] is put much more boldly by Peter Dawkins: 'The aims of The C.R.C. and the Rosicrucian fraternity, as laid out in the Rosicrucian manifestos and subsequent publications, and the great ideas and projects of Francis Bacon, are identical. [. . .] The aims are identical for the simple reason that they are both from the same source.'[16]

At this point I must radically disagree with Peter Dawkins. As we have suggested, the impulses of Francis Bacon may be regarded as identical with the impulses of James I, or with one side of this dual figure of James, but *not* with those of Christian Rosenkreutz. This error has so far been spread in two different ways. On the one hand by those who have mistakenly understood Rudolf Steiner to say that Christian Rosenkreutz directly inspired Shakespeare and Bacon—which, if true, would justify one in calling the impulses of Christian Rosenkreutz and Bacon identical. On the other by those who, ignoring the existence of any real Christian Rosenkreutz,[17] declare not just that the impulses of Bacon and Rosenkreutz are identical, but that *they* are identical, that they are one and the same person.

Those impulses of James I, which can be seen as identical with those of Francis Bacon, are in no way identical with those of Christian Rosenkreutz—they are even at times directly opposed to them. This is the whole paradox or dual nature of James, who, as an initiate, at times seems very close to the greater workings of Christian Rosenkreutz, as we witness so clearly in the later plays of Shakespeare,[18] and at times seems to work in a way quite counter to this spirit. This is all too obvious when we think of Freemasonry, for which James is such a key figure; and through James, Bacon. Freemasonry at best, at its unsullied original source, is no doubt allied and in harmony with Rosicrucianism. But in its darker, more decadent and politically manipulative aspects, it is sharply at odds with true Rosicrucianism.[19] It is at best naïve, and at worst a deliberate attempt to deceive, to say that Freemasonry *is* Rosicrucianism, just as it is equally untrue to say that Francis Bacon *is* Christian Rosenkreutz.

And slowly we become aware of the extraordinary claims Dawkins makes for Bacon. Who is *not* Francis Bacon in Dawkins's eyes? Shakespeare, James I and now Christian Rosenkreutz were all, according to Dawkins, *actually* Francis Bacon (James I not only through Bacon supposedly having inspired the King James Bible, but also because, according to Dawkins, Bacon was the secret son of Queen Elizabeth I, making him the rightful heir to the throne of England, and James I an impostor on that throne[20]). One cannot help but be reminded of Blake's Four Zoas: Urizen, Tharmas, Los and Luvah. Urizen, who for Blake was all too evident in the work of Francis Bacon, usurped the roles of the other three. Urizen does, of course, most certainly have his part to play in a balanced picture of the whole, but his claim to be the single figure, responsible for everything, is not only untrue, but a blatant attempt to usurp.

It is perhaps not without significance that Peter Dawkins denies that Shakespeare—actor and man of the theatre—

wrote Shakespeare's plays, preferring to see them as the product of Bacon's more aristocratic wisdom. Dawkins's picture—where everyone is Francis Bacon—whatever else we may say about it, presents us with a terrible story-line; unless we should laugh at the ridiculousness of it, as we do at Bottom in *A Midsummer Night's Dream*, when he wishes to play *all* the roles.[21]

Bacon, like Urizen, does have a major role to play in the drama of the time, but, if we see this rightly, the drama and interrelation between the characters is far more subtle and intricate than in Dawkins's monotheistic, Bacon-is-all portrayal.

In Britain at the end of the 16th and the beginning of the 17th Century, there are not one but three main characters—William Shakespeare, Francis Bacon and James I—working in the spheres of art, science and religion, respectively. (See their three frontispieces: plates 13, 14, 15 & 16.) Shakespeare and Bacon are both inspired by James I, their patron, accounting for the kinship between them. Yet King James, born under Gemini, has a double nature, which is expressed through his inspiration of *both* Shakespeare and Bacon, so that these two are in another sense opposites. The unambiguous blessing of Shakespeare's work is not at all to be found in Bacon's work, with its undeniable thrust towards materialism.

Living at the same time as these three, working invisibly from the continent, is the individuality of Christian Rosenkreutz, with whom James, as inspirer, is undoubtedly in some way connected, but by no means identical. This influence even extends as far as Bacon.[22] But Bacon's work is by no means synonymous with Rosicrucianism, and there is much in it of a markedly different character, which sets it in stark opposition to the whole stream of spirituality flowing from Central Europe. Shakespeare's work, on the other hand, is highly responsive to this influence. This drama is in many ways one which is still being played out, and whose end is still uncertain. It is, as I have said, a rather closed story, if all the main characters are merely Francis Bacon in disguise. The only possible dénouement in Dawkins's version is for everyone finally to unveil themselves, and to reveal that they have no identity of their own, that they have all simply been puppets in the hands of their great ventriloquist-master, Francis Bacon.

In dramatic terms, this does not make for a very interesting plot. In spiritual (and human) terms, one might well ask what kind of significance Dawkins is trying to ascribe to Bacon, by seeing him not only as Francis Bacon, but also William Shakespeare, Christian Rosenkreutz, Johann Valentin Andreae,[23] Edmund Spenser, Christopher Marlowe and others;[24] as having been responsible for the achievements of King James, such as the King James Bible and the renewal of Freemasonry, and as having been the one who, by rights, should have been King of England.[25] The boundlessness of these claims should make it no surprise when we hear where they are finally headed, though it nevertheless *does* come as a surprise. 'The master soul who was Francis Bacon', says Dawkins, 'is known today as the Lord of Civilization and Avatar of the Aquarian Age.'[26] The exact nature of this claim becomes clear a few lines later, when Dawkins speaks of 'The Master Jesus, Avatar of the Piscean Age.' In other words, what Christ—in his words 'the Master Jesus'—has been for people until now, Francis Bacon is to be from this time—or from his time—forward. This explains why in his preface Dawkins counters the fact that Bacon has often been held responsible for many of the ills of modern science and modern society by saying: 'We might just as well accuse the Buddha, or the Christ, or Mohammed, for the many evils that have been promulgated by people the world over who have claimed to be following the teachings of those great masters of wisdom and compassion.'[27]

I do not wish to try and address this final assertion. What I do wish to point out is that it is the apex and culmination of an edifice, built on a whole number of previous assertions, which simply cannot stand up.

Like Blake's Urizen, Bacon must be brought down to his rightful size, set in the right perspective. He is *not* William Shakespeare, whose plays grew out of a lifetime completely devoted to theatre, in every particular—a life very different from the courtly, political, philosophical one of Francis Bacon. He is *not* James I, as we have addressed. Francis Bacon himself, who venerated James, would perhaps have been more surprised and shocked than anyone at the modern denigration of James, and the supposition that he, Bacon, was the source and not the vehicle of what streamed spiritually from King James.[28] And nor was Bacon, in any sense whatsoever, Christian Rosenkreutz. He was Francis Bacon.

Bacon's influence, through what lives in his philosophical works, on modern thought, modern science, modern Freemasonry and modern society, has been, and still is, immense. As Adrian Gilbert says, doubting that Bacon wrote Shakespeare on account of the sheer scale of Bacon's own works: 'It seems scarcely possible that he could have found the time to write the collected works of Shakespeare—his known achievements were monumental.'[29] Nevertheless, they are also highly problematic.

We cannot just escape from the problematic nature of Bacon's work by saying that he was also everybody else. Bacon has one part to play in a greater drama. It is, in fact, only when we become aware of the very *different* roles played by Bacon, Shakespeare and James I, and also by Christian Rosenkreutz, that we begin to wake up to the real nature of this drama of modern times, in which we are still living.

***

The picture of Shakespeare and Bacon both being inspired by the initiate in King James, is a markedly different one from that which sees Bacon as the prime mover behind these three. But we must go one step further. The picture Rudolf Steiner gives is of the initiate in James not merely inspiring Francis Bacon and William Shakespeare, but also inspiring Jakob Boehme in Central Europe, and also the almost unknown Jesuit poet Jakob Balde.[30] What does this add to our understanding of the riddle surrounding Bacon and Shakespeare? In what way does this present a different picture from the Bacon-centred view of this time which is becoming increasingly popular?

Much of the popular spiritual literature we have been referring to must not only be described as Bacon-centred, but also as rather uncomfortably British-centred. In Peter Dawkins's eyes, Francis Bacon was the real author of the Rosicrucian tracts of Johann Valentin Andreae, and was the real Christian Rosenkreutz, described by Andreae as 'a German, the chief and original of our Fraternity'.[31] Dawkins is not alone in seeing continental Rosicrucianism as originating in Britain. Frances Yates, in her hugely influential book *The Rosicrucian Enlightenment*, besides very valuable historical research, expresses her conviction that the whole of continental Rosicrucianism ultimately goes back not to Bacon, but to his compatriot John Dee: 'The major influence behind the German Rosicrucian movement was undoubtedly John Dee.' (!)[32] This movement is therefore 'in one sense an export of the Elizabethan period and of the inspirations behind it'. She even believes the *name* Rosicrucianism to have stemmed

either from Dee's work, the *Monas Hieroglyphica*, or from the
rose red cross of St. George on the English flag. 'In any case,'
comments Yates, 'the name of the movement belongs, I
believe, to its English side.'[32] This view of the originating role
in continental spirituality of British figures such as Francis
Bacon and John Dee is shared by other writers such as Joy
Hancox,[33] Robert Lomas and Adrian Gilbert. All of these
writers deny the existence of an original Christian Rosenkreutz, founder of the stream of Rosicrucianism in Central
Europe, believing that everything attributed to this stream
actually stemmed from Britain.

It is not only in regard to Roscrucianism, however, that
books such as the ones I have mentioned, are 'British-
centred'. In many other ways they point repeatedly to the
predominant role of Britain in the culture, spirituality and
political affairs of Europe and the world. Gilbert's *The New
Jerusalem*, for example, sets out to show how England in the
17th Century was seen as 'God's chosen country for the new
age of enlightenment then dawning', with London its literal
'New Jerusalem', St. Paul's its Temple of Solomon, the Stone
of Scone in Westminster Abbey as Solomon's throne, and
James I, as portrayed in the writings of Francis Bacon, as the
Solomon sitting on that throne. The picture Rudolf Steiner
gives of this time reveals this British-centred view, even this
view of James I, as a one-sided one.

When Rudolf Steiner speaks about James I, as we saw earlier, he describes the extraordinary phenomenon that James,
'one of the greatest, most gigantic spirits of the British realm',
the inspirer of 'the utterly British philosopher Francis Bacon',
is *also* the inspirer of 'Shakespeare, working across so strongly
into Central Europe', and of Jakob Boehme, who 'transforms
the whole inspiration into the soul substance of Central
Europe'.[34] This is the almost unbelievable dual nature of

James—that as well as standing with Bacon behind the development of a very British-centred cultural, political and economic life, both in its occult (e.g. Freemasonic) and its public manifestations, he is at the same time 'linked by underground channels to the whole of the rest of European culture'.

Not only this, but Steiner makes it clear that, left to itself, the purely British, or nowadays Anglo-American element, bears within it a potentially overpowering tendency towards materialism and commercialism. The impulse in James through which he connects with all the spirituality of Central Europe offers the utterly necessary and health-bringing balance to this tendency within British cultural life.

We have seen how, within British cultural life, a far richer picture reveals itself when, rather than seeing Francis Bacon as the arch-orchestrator, we consider the more diverse con-stellation of the *three* hugely significant individuals of that time: William Shakespeare, Francis Bacon and James I. So too a greater and far more diverse picture is revealed when we observe this interlinking of British culture with the spirituality of Central Europe, for example with the stream of Christian Rosenkreutz, rather than seeing Central European spirituality and Rosicrucianism merely as tributaries from the stream of Francis Bacon and John Dee in Britain.

Reconciling Britain and Central Europe

The purely British element depends to a very great extent on tradition. Freemasonry, for example, as it readily acknowl-edges, reconstitutes what existed in ancient occult traditions and knowledge. The fact is often commended, for example, that 'Roslin', seen as of central importance within British spirituality, means: 'ancient knowledge passed down the generations'.[35] In Hebrew, 'Kabbalah', also accorded a certain centrality within British esotericism, likewise means the 'received wisdom'.[36]

In its true form, Central European spirituality, by contrast, has more to do with a striving for direct, present experience and knowledge of the spiritual worlds. Rudolf Steiner frequently alludes to this, for example in the first lecture where he speaks of James I:

> In Central Europe [...] one strives more, and had to strive more to reach up out of one's own spiritual capacities to spiritual cognition, to a cognition of the spiritual worlds. People have therefore leant less on that which comes from elsewhere, namely from older occult schools. We can go back through the centuries, to the beginning of the 17th Century, and we find there—namely in England, over Scotland and Ireland—less over Ireland—but spread out over Scotland such occult groups, which have transplanted into themselves what occult knowledge was in the oldest times, though they have altered it in a certain way.[37]

Steiner is not, however, merely favouring the latter kind of spirituality over the former. He developed his spiritual science on the foundations of Goethe's contribution to science, which can be seen as a development or metamorphosis of the science inaugurated by Bacon, so that this becomes capable of apprehending the living, organic world. Steiner spent 14 years editing Goethe's scientific work, and called him 'the Copernicus and the Kepler of the organic world'.[38] And yet Steiner says the following about the relationship of Goethe's science to the science born in Britain—in this case Darwin's—with the greater attention it pays to the past and to history:

Two streams have arisen in modern science; one of these I have called Goetheanism, the other Darwinism. If you study everything I have written, from the very beginning, you will see that I [have] never failed to recognize the profound significance of Darwinism [...] To understand Darwin [...] one has to make a synthesis of all the laws discovered in the past. To understand Goethe, one has to rise above this to laws which are ever new in earth existence. Both are necessary. It is not Darwinism that is the problem, nor Goetheanism, but the fact that people want to follow one or the other rather than one *and* the other.[39]

Steiner speaks of this same need to harmonize the spiritual gifts of Britain and Central Europe, I believe, when he says: 'Our task is to bridge the gulf between the Freemasons and the Rosicrucians. The work is difficult, but it must be done.'[40]

Rosicrucianism, as I have pointed out, is to be seen as having its origins more in Central Europe, and Freemasonry in Britain. Christian Rosenkreutz is described in the *Fama* as 'a German', the Rosicrucian manifestos emerged in Germany, and the stream of science running through the likes of Joachim Jungius and Goethe, culminated, one might say, in Rudolf Steiner, who was able to develop Rosicrucianism further in the 20th Century. A different stream of science emerges in Britain, as does Freemasonry, in both of which James I and Francis Bacon play such influential roles.

What Steiner is speaking about, therefore, when he speaks of the harmonizing of these two streams, and their collaboration, is nothing less than the overturning—or overcoming—of the events of the first half of the 20th Century, which witnessed the nightmare reality when Britain and Central Europe do *not* collaborate.

James I may be seen as having had the same wish for

collaboration and reconciliation as Rudolf Steiner, but from the perspective of the other side of the English Channel. James I, connected in the deepest possible way with all the ancient traditions of spirituality, of such importance in Britain, even being the prime figure behind their reappearance in his day, at the same time connects himself to the more *present* spirituality of Central Europe. He 'brings in a *new* element', and this he does by 'continuously inoculating into the substance of the British people [...] something that is linked by underground channels to the whole of the rest of European culture'. And it is precisely this 'new element', which gives the British people what 'they must not lose if they are not to fall utterly into materialism'.[41]

There are many other examples one could point to of this marriage between the cultures of Britain and Central Europe. Shakespeare, Blake and Coleridge spring quickly to mind.[42] I know of no better contemporary one than a book by the architect Christopher Day, entitled: *Consensus Design—Socially inclusive process.*[43] Architecture has been the key art of the freemasons, with their now outdated habits of secrecy. The title of Day's book shows his aim to overcome any such tendency within architecture. His method of doing this, furthermore, is one which is deeply indebted to Goethean science, as developed in the British cultural climate by Dr Margaret Colquhoun.[44] Finally, the book carries a Foreword by Prince Charles, an upholder of the best of the spirit of tradition in Britain, written from St James's Palace, in which he allies himself to the 'new breakthroughs in the area of science' which lie behind 'this wonderful and unique book'.

Sadly, however, we also find many examples of this not happening, of impulses from Britain *not* wishing to ally themselves with spiritual impulses that have arisen in Central Europe, at best merely being ignorant of them, or at worst deliberately denying their existence, and assuming their cultural and spiritual riches as their own.

We are becoming ever less naive with regard to Anglo-American intentions to draw other cultures into their own sphere of influence and to paint everything, as it were, with their one brush. Rudolf Steiner describes this as being a definite spiritual intention of certain power-groups within the Anglo-American (Anglo-Saxon) world. He speaks in particular of the intentions of these Anglo-American power groups to assume as their own the great spiritual resources of Central Europe: 'For this is the intention of the Anglo-Saxon [Anglo-American] world: to completely eradicate the truth of the development of spiritual science in Central Europe, and to set itself in its place.'[44]

I believe this also characterizes the gesture—by no means just an amusing curiosity of literature—of replacing everybody, most notably William Shakespeare and Christian Rosenkreutz, with Francis Bacon.[46]

Chapter Five

GREAT BRITAIN'S SOLOMON

History has left a major clue regarding the riddle of King James, which will offer us, in the end, another perspective from which to view many of the themes of the last chapter.

At every stage of his life, from his birth right up until his death, comparisons were made between King James and King Solomon.

His death, when it came, was described to people (by Bishop Williams) as follows: 'With lords and servants kneeling on one side, his archbishops, bishops and other of his chaplains on the other [...] without pangs or convulsions at all, *Solomon slept.*'[1]

The same Bishop Williams gave the sermon at King James's funeral. It was later published under the title: *Great Britain's Solomon*, and was a direct and lengthy comparison of King James and King Solomon. It begins: 'I dare presume to say you never read in your lives of two kings more fully paralleled amongst themselves, and better distinguished from all other kings besides themselves.'[2]

The frontispiece to King James's *Workes*, published in 1616, bears a single quotation, from the Bible, where God says to Solomon: 'I have given thee a wise and understanding heart.' (See Plate 16)

When James made his formal entry into Edinburgh, aged only 13, a central scene from King Solomon's life was acted out in from of him.[3] (The scene of King Solomon's judgement as to which of two women was the true mother of a child.) And if the comparison was not yet made at the time of

James's birth, it certainly came to be made *about* his birth, albeit mockingly. The King of France, referring to Mary Queen of Scots's affair with David Riccio, quipped that James was indeed: 'Solomon, son of David.' [4]

It has rarely, if ever, been pointed out—at least in recent times—that both Bacon *and* Shakespeare explicitly make this comparison between James and Solomon. Francis Bacon continually makes it, both in his dedications and letters to James, and within his works themselves. For example he dedicated *Novum Organon* to James, 'resembling Solomon as you do in most respects', and clearly intended 'King Solamona' in *New Atlantis* to symbolize James.[5] Shakespeare, as we saw, describes Cymbeline and King James with the same image. Cymbeline is 'the lofty cedar', James in *Henry VIII* will: '...like a mountain cedar, reach his branches / To all the plains about him.' Were we better versed in the Bible we would immediately recognize the connection of these 'cedars' with King Solomon. Solomon's 'countenance is as Lebanon, excellent as the cedars' (*Song of Songs*). For Solomon's Temple there was no more important building material. In the Holy of Holies ('the oracle'): 'All was cedar; there was no stone seen.'[6] In its centre lay the 'ark of the covenant upon an altar which was of cedar'.[7]

Shakespeare almost certainly also made the comparison on a further occasion. The lines underneath King James's effigy, on the left-hand page of the frontispiece to James's *Workes*, (1616), are attributed to Shakespeare.[8] The line 'But knowledge makes the king most like his maker' clearly invites a connection with the quotation about King Solomon on the opposite page. (See Plates 15 and 16.)

That Bacon and Shakespeare make the comparison should surely lead us to question whether this was all merely empty flattery of the King.

When we look more closely we find that the points of similarity are indeed remarkable. We will focus on *three* of these from, roughly, the beginning, middle and end of Solomon's reign. With each one we shall look first at the external evidence, and then at what our research from the previous chapters may add to this.

The first and foremost connection between the two rulers was regarding their learning and wisdom. Soon after the young Solomon became king, God appeared to him in a dream, saying: 'Ask what shall I give thee?' (1 Kings 3, Verse 5). Solomon asked for 'an understanding heart [...] to judge thy people, that I may discern between good and bad'. God replied: 'Behold, I have done according to thy words: lo, I have given thee a wise and an understanding heart.' From that moment on Solomon's wisdom became proverbial. In the words of the Bible:

> And God gave Solomon wisdom and understanding exceeding much, and largeness of heart, even as the sand that is on the sea shore.
> And he spake three thousand proverbs: and his songs were a thousand and five.
> And there came of all people to hear the wisdom of Solomon. (1 Kings 4, 29–34)

King James also displayed remarkable faculties of learning and understanding from a very young age. Besides poetry, theology and history he studied with his tutors 'geometry and physics, logic and rhetoric, dialectic and astronomy'. Visitors, before whom the *eight-year-old* James was made to demonstrate his abilities, described him as: 'The sweetest sight in Europe for strange and extraordinary gifts of ingine, judgement, memory and language.'[9] They witnessed the King translate, spontaneously, a chapter of the Bible from Latin into French and then from French into English '...as well as few men could have added anything to his translation'.[10]

Shakespeare commented on James's learning, in his frontispiece verse, and Robert Fludd spoke of 'his most Excellent and learned Majestie'.[11] Isaac Casaubon, 'one of the most brilliant scholars of his time', considered by his friend Joseph Scaliger to be 'the most learned man in Europe',[12] said of James: '*He is a lover of learning to a degree beyond belief,* his judgement of books, old and new, is such as would become a professed scholar rather than a mightie prince.'[13] (My emphasis.)

Francis Bacon went way beyond all of these remarks, saying: 'There hath not been since Christ's time any king or temporal monarch, which hath been so learned in all literature and erudition, divine and human.'[14]

James, like Solomon, wrote poetry and many books,[15] besides being 'the principal Mover and Author' of what is known as the 'King James Bible'.

The *quality* of James's wisdom may also be compared with Solomon's. Solomon's wisdom was not won over years of hardship and experience but was an innate, God-given gift. King James possessed a similar kind of 'foolish wisdom'— indicated by the King of France's famous epithet: 'the wisest fool in Christendom'.

This first comparison is *hugely* enhanced when we relate it to our discoveries of the last chapter. Solomon's prime characteristic, from an esoteric perspective is that *despite* his immense wisdom, despite being the one predestined to build the Temple, and being able to perceive the exact form and measurements it needed, he himself was not able to build it. The person who *was* able to do this was the 'Master Builder' from Tyre, Hiram Abiff. Solomon's wisdom is able to perceive, in the heavenly world, what needs to come about, but is completely unable to fashion this in the earthly world.

Rudolf Steiner relates this difference between Hiram and Solomon to the older polarity of Cain and Abel, and describes it as follows:

> From Abel's line comes Solomon [. . .] He was endowed with the wisdom of the world and all the attributes of calm, clear, objective wisdom. This wisdom can be expressed in words which go straight to the human heart and can uplift a person, *but it is unable to produce anything tangible of a technical nature, in art or science.* [16] (My emphasis.)

When we turn to James I, we recall Rudolf Steiner saying that what is important about him is not to be found by looking at his own achievements: 'Even what he himself wrote does not give us any clear insight into his soul.' In order to observe the true story of his achievement we must direct our gaze, in fact, to the works of others—of Francis Bacon, William Shakespeare, Jakob Boehme and Jakob Balde—who worked out of his inspiration; who, we might say, made this inspiration manifest on earth.

Everything about James's life shows it to be 'Solomonic', in the way we have described, to the fullest possible extent. His whole way of working, as patron, attests to this. Not only with the four individuals just mentioned, but also with Inigo Jones, John Donne and others (see Chapter Six), we see him setting something into motion, initiating it, but not carrying it out himself.

The second aspect relates to what must be seen as the *central* achievement of Solomon's life and reign, the building of Solomon's Temple.

There is clearly little real value in any comparison between King Solomon and King James unless it can answer the question: Is there anything, in the life and achievement of King James, comparable to the building of this Temple?

Outer research provides two striking answers to this. In the Banqueting House at Whitehall, completed in the reign of James's son, Charles I, several huge and grandiose paintings by Rubens depict, somewhat absurdly to our modern eyes: 'The Apotheosis of King James', with such titles as: 'The Judgement of Solomon: James I recreates the Empire of Great Britain' and 'The Reign of Solomon: The Golden Age of James I.'

Sir Roy Strong, in the final section of his book *Britannia Triumphans—Whitehall and the Temple of Solomon,*[17] provides convincing arguments that the Whitehall Banqueting House was originally intended as part of a far larger scheme, a wholly new Whitehall Palace. Strong states: 'The plan of Whitehall Palace was composed of mystical geometry that posterity might know that here lived the Solomonic Kings of Great Britain', and that, although it was only fully conceived after King James died in 1625, 'the central idea of [the] new palace must have been at the back of Inigo Jones's mind as early as 1619'.

Strong admits he has no written evidence or drawings to prove his thesis, but says:

What I would like to pose is the hypothesis that the building and the ceiling are only parts of a vast scheme for a new palace centring on the Solomonic idea and that this was in everybody's mind from the first discussions back in James I's reign. Whatever was hammered out in 1629 between Rubens, Charles I and Inigo Jones took place within this overall context, that of Solomon and his Temple. The iconography of the ceiling is therefore much more than the localized decoration of one room.

What Strong is suggesting, which he backs up with striking geometrical and architectural parallels, is that there was an intention, under James, to make a new palace, which would be a *physical* equivalent of the Temple of Solomon.[18]

The second achievement of James which we can equate with Solomon's Temple is conceived on a greater scale than any building in stone, however grandly designed.

As we saw in the last chapter, evidence has begun to emerge—as seen in Robert Lomas's *The Invisible College*—that James I is to be regarded as largely responsible for the establishment and reconstituting of modern Freemasonry.[19] This gives clear confirmation to what Rudolf Steiner said of James I in 1916, that he 'stands at the beginning of the renewal of the Brotherhoods'.

Freemasonry, in its own terms, is nothing other than the attempt 'to *rebuild the Temple of Solomon*'. As Peter Dawkins writes: 'In Freemasonic lore it is the rebuilding of the Temple of Solomon by a fraternity in learning dedicated to charity [...] led by a "Second Solomon" [...] which lies at the heart of their Mysteries.[20] Or, in Emil Bock's words: 'The Freemasons trace their symbolism back to Solomon and refer to their cultic premises as Temples of Solomon.'[21]

Through the establishing of modern Freemasonry, therefore, King James not only does something analogous to the rebuilding of Solomon's Temple, but something referred to as such by name by all Freemasons.

Based on our previous discoveries, we may take this parallel even further. The immense spiritual inspiration, which at the turn of the 16th and 17th centuries found its focal point in James I, is given form and expression *in Britain* in the artistic works of Shakespeare and the scientific works of Bacon. Solomon's wisdom itself, we remember, 'is unable to produce anything tangible of a technical nature, in art or science.'

If the impulse James gave to Freemasonry remains for the most part hidden from outer view, the inspiration working through James is made immediately and publicly manifest through the works of Bacon and Shakespeare, a cultural edifice on earth, we might say, whose immensity and influence could hardly be greater. It is not, I believe, too far-fetched to note that this edifice, like King Solomon's Temple, also has two pillars, polar opposites to one another. In Solomon's Temple these were known as Jachin and Boaz.[22] Peter Dawkins, with his sure sense of the common inspiration behind Bacon and Shakespeare (though we differ radically, as I have shown, when it comes to naming the source of this inspiration), also clearly notes this connection. Of the four brief headings Dawkins gives for the aims of the 'Francis Bacon Research Trust', the final one is: 'Bacon and Shakespeare—Twin Beacons—Pillars of Solomon's Temple.'[23] If we refer these two pillars all the way back to their origin in the Garden of Eden they become the Tree of Life and the Tree of Knowledge. It is easy enough to see the connection of these two trees, and their polarity, with the works of Shakespeare and Bacon.

The final parallel, though, between Solomon and James, refuses to allow us to relax in relation to this polarity. For when we look at the end of Solomon's life, we discover a feature about the 'Solomonic' which we cannot possibly afford to ignore, namely that it is, to a highly disturbing degree, *double-edged*.

The early part of Solomon's life bears all the signature of one ordained by God. God speaks to him in sleep and bestows on him the gift of wisdom. In the middle part of his life, Solomon then achieves his world-historic task, the building of the Temple, and this receives God's blessing. He achieves this by *working together* with Hiram, the representative of the opposite, though complementary stream to his own.

From that point on, Solomon's life, as the Bible describes it, runs directly counter to God's will.

In the 'Temple Legend', describing the actual building of the Temple, this drastic change within Solomon takes place just *before* the building is completed. The legend tells how Balkis, the Queen of Sheba, who is betrothed to Solomon, at a single glance falls in love with Hiram, the Master Builder. Solomon's jealousy is such that he does not interfere when he learns of a plan to murder Hiram, and thus he colludes in the act. According to the legend, the darker aspects of Solomon, and his fall from grace, are therefore directly linked with his enmity with Hiram.

The version in the Bible is that the moment the Temple has been completed, God appears once again to Solomon, bearing him a twofold message. First God tells him: 'I have consecrated this house which you have built, to receive my Name for all time, and my eyes and heart shall be fixed on it for ever.'[24] Then He warns Solomon:

> But [...] if you go and serve other gods and prostrate yourselves before them [...] I will renounce this house which I have consecrated [...] and Israel shall become a byword and an object lesson among all peoples. And this house will become a ruin; every passer-by will be appalled and gasp at the sight of it.[25]

God must have seen what was coming, for the rest of Solomon's life was the exact fulfilment of everything he had been urged *not* to do:

> King Solomon was a lover of women, and besides Pharaoh's daughter he married many foreign women [...] from the

nations with whom the Lord had forbidden the Israelites to
inter-marry [...] his wives turned his heart to follow other
gods, and he did not remain wholly loyal to the Lord his
God.

God furiously rejects Solomon: 'Because you have done this
[...] I will tear the kingdom from you.'

The uncanny outer parallels with King James continue, for
God adds: 'Nevertheless, for the sake of your father David I
will not do this in your day; I will tear it out of your son's
hand.'[26]

With James too, it was not during his own reign, but in that
of his *son*, Charles I, that the destruction—or division—of his
kingdom comes about, with the English Civil War, leading to
the execution of the King on a balcony outside—where
else?—the Whitehall Banqueting House.

Once again, though, the parallels run far deeper than
merely external ones. In Chapter Two we saw how James I's
spiritual influence has a *double* nature that is extremely similar
to Solomon's. Rudolf Steiner describes James on the one
hand in the most positive of lights, as the bearer of an impulse
which Britain and the English-speaking world 'must never
lose if it is not to fall utterly into materialism'. This aspect of
James's activity, and one cannot help but think in this regard
of the works of Shakespeare, particularly his later plays, strikes
one as being in the closest possible alignment with true
Rosicrucianism. It is easy to suppose that Solomon-James, in
this aspect, works directly in co-operation with Hiram/
Christian Rosenkreutz.

On the other hand Steiner describes James as representing
an influence that must often be seen as sinister in the
extreme. This aspect of James is connected with materialism,
with Freemasonry and with the occult manipulation of world

politics, particularly by the powers behind the Anglo-American elites. (Although this may once have been disregarded by people as fiction, recent political events, particularly since 11 September 2001, have alerted an unprecedented number of people throughout the world to these kinds of goings-on.) At least in terms of scientific materialism and Freemasonry we cannot avoid connecting this aspect of James with the work of Francis Bacon.[27] This aspect, at its worst, like the Solomon of the Temple legend, can even reveal itself, despite appearances, to be in direct enmity with Hiram, or with the true source of Rosicrucianism.[28]

The parallels between King Solomon and King James, far from being a matter of empty flattery, thus reveal themselves not only to be wide-ranging and consistent, but also to have a profound, occult base.

So powerful are the echoes between the two rulers that it is tempting to imagine that in King James there lived the same individual who had once lived as King Solomon. I am in no position, however, to assert such a thing, and the truth may prove to be very different. What we certainly can say, though, beyond any shadow of a doubt, is that James I has a most profound connection with the Solomonic *stream*, and must be seen, at the very least, as one of the foremost representatives of that stream.

When we remember that Rudolf Steiner stated that Christian Rosenkreutz was a reincarnation of the individual who had once lived as Hiram Abiff, 'Master Builder' of the Temple,[29] a startling picture presents itself. For Christian Rosenkreutz, according to Rudolf Steiner, was also incarnated on earth, in Europe, at the turn of the 16th and 17th centuries. Thus the picture emerges of there being not one but two huge spiritual influences at this time. From Britain,

'Great Britain's Solomon', King James, inspires the works of Shakespeare, Bacon, Boehme and Balde, while in Central Europe the reincarnated Hiram, Christian Rosenkreutz, inspires the more hidden stream of Rosicrucianism.

The picture of James as this Solomonic figure is confirmed in a further remark by Rudolf Steiner which I have not yet mentioned. The God-given wisdom of Solomon, unable to engage practically with the earthly realm, is also designated by Steiner as 'the ancient priestly wisdom'. This is to be contrasted with the creativity and activity of Hiram, but is not only to be understood in a literal sense:

> What is involved here has nothing to do with churches and creeds. Priestliness can show itself in the most completely secular [people]. Even what manifests today as science, that holds sway in many cultural groups, is nothing other than what is known in Freemasonry terms as the priestly element...[30]

In a lecture of 1919 Steiner firmly links James with this priestly, Solomonic stream: 'There was one person, James I, who still made an effort to save the old dominion of the priesthood; and *one best understands James I if one looks on him as a conservator—a man who was trying to conserve the rule of the priesthood*, although his plans were thwarted by others.'[31] (My emphasis.)

The implications of this are profound and far-reaching, for what it tells of the spiritual interrelationship of Britain (or the West) and Central Europe is still completely valid today. This could be explored in detail but it would lead us too far from our present task of exploring the great riddles posed by these three individuals—Shakespeare, Bacon and James—almost exactly 400 years ago.

Chapter Six

TOWARDS A RECONSIDERATION OF JAMES I

A friend has commented that this is a slightly ridiculous chapter-title, as the whole book has been an attempt to reconsider James I. I have kept the title however, for unlike Chapter Two for example, this chapter is intended to show what purely documentary evidence may add to our picture of King James as someone with far more going on under the surface than was visible in his outer life.

During the research for this book I have stumbled across various curious pieces of information relating to King James. These are not to be found, for the most part, in the many biographies of King James, but are scattered around, often in works about other authors. I put them together here, in no particular order, as a small contribution towards a reconsideration of King James. If, in time, others are able to add to these, revealing their incompleteness, so much the better.

1. Acquaintances and book dedications

Tycho Brahe

As James VI of Scotland, James visited the hugely significant figure of Tycho Brahe, astronomer and alchemist, on his island of Hven, on 20 March 1590. James wrote three sonnets about Tycho, one of which, having spoken of the role of the planets, ends:

Then great is Ticho who, by this his booke,
Commandment doth over these commanders brooke.

James may well also have met Tycho on other occasions,
during the winter of 1589/90, which he spent at the Court of
Copenhagen. (He had married Queen Anne of Denmark in
Oslo, on 23 November 1589, after which they spent their
honeymoon in Hamlet's Elsinore.) James would have been
aware of Tycho through his tutor George Buchanan, who had
also taught Montaigne. Buchanan had met Tycho, corre-
sponded with him, and James had found Buchanan's portrait
hanging in Tycho's library.

Johannes Kepler

Possibly through what he had heard of King James from
Tycho Brahe, Kepler dedicated his main work *Harmonice
Mundi* (Harmony of the World) to King James, saying that he
knew of:

> ...no more suitable patron for my work on the heavenly
> harmonies, recalling Pythagoras and Plato, than the great
> King who, in his own achievements, has shown his special
> fondness for the philosophy of Plato.[1]

Our picture of Kepler, like that of Brahe and King James
himself, is constantly being extended. Frances Yates says that
Kepler 'moved in Andreae's cicle', perhaps in view of Kepler's
friendship with Christoph Besold, a close friend and collea-
gue of Johann Valentin Andreae. Yates ends by saying:
'Kepler's association with the Rosicrucian world is so close
that one might almost call him a heretic from
Rosicrucianism.'[2]

Rudolf II (and his court in Prague)

Something of James's connection to the culture of Central Europe, or certainly to Bohemia, was observable in his links with the court of Rudolf II in Prague. Comparatively little attention has been paid to these.

In 1608, Emperor Rudolf II's brother, Matthias, usurped three of his kingdoms: Austria, Hungary and Moravia.

King James's support for his fellow-ruler may perhaps therefore be seen in his 1609 dedication of a book to Rudolf. The book—*A Premonition to all Most Mightie Monarches, Kings, Free Princes, and States of Christendome*—is dedicated first and foremost to '...the most sacred and invincible Prince, Rudolphe the II by Gods Clemencie Elect Emperor of the Romans; King of Germanie, Hungarie, Boheme, Dalmatie, Croatie, Slavonie &c.' In June 1609 James appointed John Barclay to personally deliver a copy of the book to Rudolf.

In the same year Rudolf sent James 'two characteristic gifts: a celestial globe and a clock.'[3]

As so often with James, we are obliged to look at what he gave his patronage to, or, conversely, what was *dedicated* to him. We hear, for example, that 'when a new Protestant church was built in Prague during the early years of the seventeenth century its greatest subscriber was King James I'. (p. 1.)

We also need to look at the connections and movements between *people* at the two courts. Tycho Brahe was, of course, Rudolf's court astronomer, as was Kepler, who dedicated his *Harmonices Mundi* to King James. In the opinion of R. J. W. Evans, 'It is not surprising that the Emperor's great favourite Kepler later received an invitation to come to the court of King James.' (p. 81.)

The 'extraordinary Dutchman Cornelius Drebbel' (see page 114), was attracted by Rudolf II away from King James's

1. From the Karlstejn
Chapel, Prague

2. James VI of Scotland (1595): 'A great enigma on the threshold of the seventeenth century.' (Rudolf Steiner)

3. James I of England (1621): 'In his position as Sovereign, James I resembled a man dressed in ill-fitting garments.' (Rudolf Steiner)

4. Francis Bacon (1623)

5. James VI & I (1615)

6. *William Shakespeare*

7. *Jakob Boehme*

'In the city of Goerlitz there is a monument of Boehme which does not in the least represent a form which could have belonged to the shoemaker of Goerlitz, but which far more reminds the observer of Shakespeare. This has been felt by many people. Dr. Steiner was once shown this likeness by friends who were with him. He said that it concealed a truth; the sculptor had been unconsciously guided in his work through the fact that there was the same inspiration behind the two individualities.' (Ernst Lehrs.)

8. *Jakob Balde (1604–1668)*   9. *Jakob Boehme (1575–1624)*

'[Rudolf Steiner] had been invited to the unveiling of the Jakob Boehme statue. Marie Steiner upset the Mayor quite considerably when she told him that it was more a statue of Shakespeare than of Jakob Boehme. But, Rudolf Steiner said, she was right in one respect, as Boehme, Shakespeare, Bacon and Balde actually all looked similar—*they had all had the same initiation teacher!' (Countess Johanna Keyserlingk.)*

10. *James I (1566–1625)*   11. *Francis Bacon (1561–1626)*

12. *William Shakespeare (1564–1616)*

13. *William Shakespeare,* The First Folio, *1623, frontispiece.*

14. *Francis Bacon*—Of the Advancement and Proficiencie of Learning, *1640, frontispiece.*

15, 16. *King James,* Workes, *1616, double frontispiece*

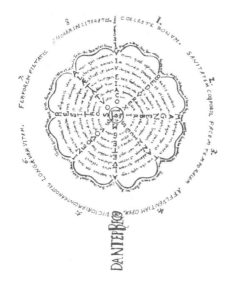

17. *Christmas Greeting to James I from Michael Maier (1612). 'Unmistakably a Rosicrucian symbol.'* (Joy Hancox)

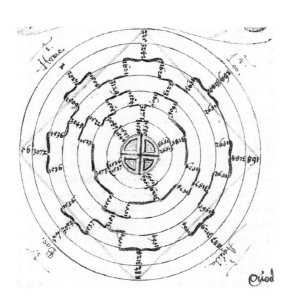

18. *'A crudely shaped rose design, with a cross in the centre, contained in the* Naometria *(1604)... The whole composition [of the* Naometria*] seems to reflect a secret alliance between Henry, King of France, James I of Great Britain and Frederick, Duke of Württemberg.'* (Frances Yates.)

1 The confidence which the Church hath in God. 8 An exhortation to behold it.

¶ To the chiefe Musician ‖ for the sonnes of Korah, a song vpon Alamoth.

GOD is our refuge and strength: a very present helpe in trouble.

2 Therefore will not we feare, though the earth be remoued: and though the mountaines be caried into † the midst of the sea.

3 Though the waters thereof roare, and be troubled, though the mountaines shake with the swelling thereof. Selah.

4 There is a riuer, the streames wherof shall make glad the citie of God: the holy place of the Tabernacles of the most High.

5 God is in the midst of her: she shal not be moued: God shall helpe her, † and that right early.

6 The heathen raged, the kingdomes were moued: he vttered his voyce, the earth melted.

7 The LORD of hosts is with vs; the God of Jacob is † our refuge. Selah.

8 Come, behold the workes of the LORD, what desolations hee hath made in the earth.

9 He maketh warres to cease vnto the end of the earth: hee breaketh the bow, and cutteth the speare in sunder, he burneth the chariot in the fire.

10 Be still, and know that I am God: I will bee exalted among the heathen, I will be exalted in the earth.

11 The LORD of hosts is with vs; the God of Jacob is our refuge. Selah.

Shakespeare:
The King's Man?

Globe Education Spring 2003

19. *Psalm 46,* King James Bible, *(1611)*

20. Shakespeare's Globe *Education Brochure, 2003*

court to Prague. Michael Maier is another link between the two courts. Having been Rudolf's court physician he then came to England, becoming friends both with Robert Fludd (with his connections to James) and with James's own doctor, Sir William Paddy.

R. J. W. Evans offers a pertinent, extended comparison between King James and Emperor Rudolf, which begins:

> It is remarkable how much of what in isolation was merely perverse falls into place when these two sovereigns are considered together, and if James was the wisest fool in Christendom then Rudolf was perhaps the sanest madman. (p. 80.)

There follow comparisons of their upbringing and education; and of their patronage and private lives: 'Their patronage was close to esotericism. Their private life was abnormal . . .'; their 'tastes and pastimes, especially the interest in occult studies, the spirit world and the machine'; their belief in the divine right of monarchy; their peace-making intentions and their political activity. As the latter has been so responsible for James's unpopularity—leading to the extreme Protestant cause desiring to explode his reputation at least as much as the Catholics desired, in the Gunpowder Plot, to explode his person—it is at least worth hearing Evans's defence of this:

> James and Rudolf each aimed to achieve a European balance of power by playing off rival forces and casting themselves for the role of international arbiter. This line of policy runs right through James's conciliatory diplomacy during the years 1618–20, which in Protestant eyes amounted to betrayal, and appears most clearly of all in his pamphlet of 1618, *The Peace-maker or Great Brittaine's Blessing.* Thus considered the Catholic Rudolf's continued refusal of

a Spanish marriage presents a strong parallel with the Protestant James's insistence on it for his son the Prince of Wales. (p. 82.)

Three out of Shakespeare's four last plays also show hints of a connection with Rudolf II and/or Bohemia. Leontes's son-in-law Florizel in *The Winter's Tale* is heir to Bohemia, where much of the play takes place. Many people have also commented on the echoes between Prospero, in *The Tempest*, being ousted by his brother after becoming over-interested in his occult studies, and Rudolf II, whose brother Matthias usurped his throne of Bohemia at exactly the time *The Tempest* was written (1610–11). A book of 1609 (by Daniel Eremita) had described how Rudolf had ruined his great gifts as ruler 'by taking up the study of art and nature, with such increasing lack of moderation that he has deserted the affairs of state for alchemists' laboratories, printers' studios and the workshops of clockmakers' (p. 45, Evans). This view was obviously shared by James's personal envoy to Rudolf, John Barclay, who wrote, according to Evans, a 'scurrilous roman à clef' about Rudolf. Prospero thus comes to be seen, fascinatingly, as combining ingredients from Rudolf II and James I.

With *Cymbeline*, I have already commented on the parallels between King Cymbeline and King James, and those between Posthumus, Cymbeline's son-in-law and Frederick (Elector Palatine), James's son-in-law. An aspect to the play I did not discuss was Cymbeline's decision, much to everyone's surprise, freely to pay tribute to the Roman Emperor. This introduces a great, freely chosen peace between Britain and Rome, the announcement of which ends the play. (The last word of the play is 'peace'.) The parallel in Shakespeare's time with this peace between King Cymbeline and Emperor

Augustus has, of course, to be seen as that between King James and the Holy Roman Emperor, Rudolf.

That James's interests also extended beyond Europe can be seen in his correspondence with the Emperor of Japan, his embassies to Russia and to India, and his involvement in America. This is not the place, however, to discuss these in any detail.

Michael Maier

Michael Maier did not, as far as I know, dedicate any volume to King James, though he dedicated *Arcana Arcanissima* to Sir William Paddy, James's physician, in 1614. Maier almost certainly met King James, although we don't know the circumstances. (Maier attended the funeral in 1612 of James's son, Prince Henry, as part of the household of James's future son-in-law, Frederick.) In the same year Maier sent James a hand-drawn Christmas card, on parchment 3 × 2 foot large, which has been described by some as a Rosicrucian symbol. (See Plate 17.)

Robert Fludd

Robert Fludd dedicated three works to King James, *A Philosophicall Key*, *Declaratio Brevis* (see 'Rosicrucianism') and, by far the most important publicly, the first part of *Utriusque Cosmi Historia* (The History of the Macrocosm). Frances Yates describes this latter dedication as follows:

> James is addressed as 'TER MAXIMUS', Emperor of the heavens and the earth, a shining ray of the divine light, to whom the truths of Nature revealed in the book are dedicated, which open a way to the heavens as by Jacob's Ladder, and are presented to the Deity on earth, King James.[4]

Fludd and James clearly enjoyed a fruitful exchange with one another. Fludd writes that he has 'ever found your most sacred majesty [...] to beholde me with the eye of your favourable benignity.' (Dedication to *A Philosophicall Key*.) Fludd describes James giving the same kind of detailed response to his work as he had given to Bacon. Regarding a certain 'alchemical experiment on wheat', for example, Fludd describes how 'it pleased his most Excellent and learned Majestie to object to me and that most rightly'.[5]

Fludd's own words give no support to the view, widely held at present, that James was opposed to Fludd. If we wish to hold this view, we must in fact *disbelieve* Fludd. Joscelyn Godwin writes that Fludd was summoned by James in 1617 to reply to accusations that had been made about *Utriusque Cosmi Historia*. Far from James going along with the accusations, the result of the meeting, in Fludd's own words, was that he: '...received from that time forward many gracious favours of him, and found him my just and kingly patron all the days of his life.'[6] (I include further comment on Fludd in the two sections of this chapter—'Hermeticism' and 'Rosicrucianism'.)

John Donne

John Donne, the full complexity and depth of whose story one feels has not yet been told, dedicated his book *Pseudo-Martyr* to King James. An early biography of Donne stated: 'In 1609 [...] the King commanded the composition of the *Pseudo-Martyr*.' (Walton, *Life of Donne*.) A later biographer comments: 'If the *Pseudo-Martyr* was not written at the King's command—and of course such authority would not in any case be spoken of in the book itself—it was at least dedicated to the King and written chiefly to win his regard.'[7]

The final chapter of Charles Williams's wonderful biography of King James[8] is called: 'The Oration of John Donne.' Williams tells us that: 'By [Donne's] own testimony he owed to James the occasion of his own soul's second birth; he owed to him his priesthood, and all that his priesthood had meant to him.'

Donne himself said of this: 'When I sit still and reckon all my old Master's royal favours to me, I return evermore to that—that he first inclined me to be a minister.' Donne added: 'I date my life from my Ministry, for I received mercy, as I received the ministry.' The way this happened tells us a tale.

Robert Carr had asked King James to make Donne a 'Clerk of the Council'. James had refused, saying: 'I know Mr Donne is a learned man, has the abilities of a learned Divine; and will prove a powerful Preacher, *and my desire is to prefer him that way.*' (My emphasis.)

In Williams's words:

> By that obstinacy Donne was driven into secret searchings of his spirit, and in those searchings he found the way of the last spiritual search. It might have happened in many ways; it did happen in that way. It is to James Stuart that the deep and sublime rhetoric of the sermons is, by occasion, due, and to him that the discovery of God which shadows and illuminates that rhetoric is also due.

After King James died, a few days before his funeral, Donne preached over his dead body. He chose for his theme the hand of the King. George Villiers may once have written to James: 'I kiss your dirty hands', but Donne's words are somewhat different: '*That Hand, which was the hand of Destinie, of Christian Destinie, of the Almighty God* [...] (It was not so hard a hand when we touched it last nor so cold a hand when we kissed it last.)'

Inigo Jones and Ben Jonson (Court Masques)

A thorough treatment of King James's cultural influence, and his connections with significant individuals, would obviously need to include discussion of those politically and spiritually complex entities, the Court Masques. Others could do this far more ably than myself.[9]

The masques were extravagantly expensive,[10] being highly elaborate technically. Cornelius Drebbel, who dedicated his 'perpetuum mobile' machine to James, was one of the people entrusted by James 'with preparing spectacular effects for his court masques.'[11] Frances Yates speculates that Robert Fludd may have co-operated with Inigo Jones on the 'perspective-scenes type of theatre' established by the Masques. The connections of Inigo Jones, the central designer and architect of the Masques, with King James, could obviously be discussed at length. Besides the Masques, his research into Stonehenge, his designs of Whitehall Palace, and many another court building, Jones also designed James's elaborate catafalque for his funeral in Westminster Abbey.

Ben Jonson is the other major player in the whole strange enterprise of the Masques. Jonson, their most famous writer, gives us, or rather the elect court audience, such lines as these, comparing Prince Henry to Oberon and James to King Arthur.

> Melt earth to sea, sea flow to air,
>   And air fly into fire,
> Whilst we in tunes to Arthur's chair
>   Bear Oberon's desire,
>   Than which there nothing can be higher,
> Save James, to whom it flies:
> But he the wonder is of tongues, of ears, of eyes.[12]

Nothing, to those of a literary inclination, can speak more fully of James's double nature, than that he was the recipient both of words such as these, and of *King Lear*.

Finally it should be noted that James, aged 22, had himself written and devised a Masque, for a marriage in Holyrood Palace, in which he began the tradition Jonson continues here of comparing his court with 'Arthur's Chair'. The comparison had a topographical reality in the context of James's Masque, for Holyrood Palace sits at the foot of Edinburgh's landmark hill of 'Arthur's Seat'.

William Harvey and William Paddy (Court Physicians)

King James's physician was Sir William Paddy, and his 'Physician Extraordinary' was Sir William Harvey, who discovered the circulation of the blood. Both were friends with another 'Fellow of the Royal College of Physicians', whom we have already spoken of: Robert Fludd,[13] who, according to Frances Yates, practised an 'unorthodox and Paracelsan type of medicine'.

Fludd and Paddy later became friends with Rudolf II's court physician, Michael Maier—'the most mysterious of the court physicians [...] Paracelsan, alchemist and reformer'.[14] Maier and Fludd both dedicated books to Paddy.

Some wise doctor might one day offer revealing insights about all these medical interconnections. They are complex, but certainly do not leave one with a sense of any horror, in the closest medical circle around King James, of what was represented by Fludd and Maier. We encounter instead, as ever, a riddling co-existence of the old and the new.

The one person who definitely does speak out against the influence of Paracelsus is Francis Bacon. The Rosicrucian pamphlet, the *Fama*, speaks in terms of the highest praise of Paracelsus, and highly negatively of Galen. This is one instance where we can see a clear divergence between the attitudes of the author of the *Fama* and of Francis Bacon. On one occasion when King James was ill, Bacon wrote to him: 'I beseech your Majesty to give me leave to make this judgement; your Majesty's recovery must be by the medicines of the Galenists and Arabians, and not of the Chemists or Paracelsians.'[15] In *The Advancement of Learning* (Book Two) Bacon also speaks scornfully of 'Paracelsus and the Alchemists.'

2. *Hermeticism*

Francis Yates points out that 'no full-scale treatment of Hermetic philosophy by an Englishman was published until the reign of James I'.[16]

In 1614 Isaac Casaubon published a work of colossal influence, (entitled *De Rebus sacris et ecclesiasticis exercitationes XVI*) in which he offered compelling evidence that the Central Hermetic text, the *Hermetica,* could not be attributed to the legendary Hermes Trismegistos himself, in Ancient Egypt, but had in fact clearly been written down *after* the time of Christ. Frances Yates describes the shattering effect of Casaubon's dating of the *Hermetica* on the whole attitude of people towards Hermeticism, and calls it 'a watershed separating the Renaissance world from the modern world'.[17]

Casaubon dedicated his book to King James, who according to Yates even encouraged Casaubon to embark on it in the first place.[18] A biography of Donne states that: 'Casaubon came to England at the King's invitation.'[19]

This has led to the view of James as a profound enemy of Hermeticism, and of people like Fludd and Maier.

This is a view which completely ignores—or denies—not only James's dual nature, but also how he was perceived at the time. For three years *after* Casaubon's book came out Robert Fludd dedicated his own *Utriusque Cosmi Historia* to King James, *as* Hermes Trismegistos, by naming him 'Ter Maximus'.[20] Speaking of Fludd's lengthy dedications to James, she comments: 'It is almost as though Fludd calls on James in these dedications as Defender of the Hermetic Faith.'[21]

Francis Bacon also specifically addresses James as Thrice-Great-Hermes: 'Your Majesty standeth invested of that triplicity, which in great veneration was ascribed to the ancient Hermes; the power and fortune of a King, the knowledge and illumination of a priest, and the learning and universality of a philosopher.'[22]

3. Rosicrucianism

As we have described in other chapters, a distinction must be made between what external evidence tells of Rosicrucianism, and calls Rosicrucianism, and those true Rosicrucians who worked completely out of the public eye, and about whom there is no documentation. I am obviously not able to speak about the latter, and any possible connections of them with James I. There are, however, several connections between James and what is externally known of Rosicrucianism, which have not previously been brought together.

In his *Declaratio Brevis,* Robert Fludd specifically discusses Rosicrucianism with King James. It is a 'Brief Declaration' to James, its full Latin title being: 'Declaratio brevis Serenissimo et Potentissimo Principe ac Domine Jacobo Magnae Britanniae [...] Regi.' In it, according to Yates, Fludd 'vindicates the Rosicrucians, and himself as attached to them, defends his philosophy as drawn from ancient and holy sources, and mentions the dedication of the Macrocosm volume to 'your Majestie immediately after God'.[23]

In 1611 Michael Maier sent King James what has often been called a 'Rosicrucian Christmas Card'. (See Plate 17) Joy Hancox says of it:

> Drawn on parchment measuring three feet by two, it consists mainly of an eight-petalled rose covered with Latin inscriptions. Encircling the petals are wishes for the King's health and prosperity. It is unmistakably a Rosicrucian symbol...[24]

The extraordinary nature of Simon Studion's *Naometria*, written in 1604, makes it very likely that it does indeed, as many have believed, contain a reflection of genuine Rosicrucian realities. Frances Yates states that several 'early students of the Rosicrucian mystery', and Johann Valentin Andreae himself, saw the *Naometria* as having 'an important bearing on the Rosicrucian movement'.

The *Naometria* describes certain events which, to my knowledge, are alluded to in no other documents of the time. It speaks of an important conference, for example, that took place in 1586, in Lüneburg, seen by some as a 'source for the Rosicrucian movement'.

'*The whole composition*' of the *Naometria*, according to Yates, '*seems to reflect a secret alliance between Henry, King of France, James I of Great Britain and Frederick, Duke of Württemberg.*' According to Simon Studion, the 'secret alliance' between these three took place in 1604—a year of enormous importance for the Rosicrucian movement. According to the *Fama Fraternitatis*, Christian Rosenkreutz's tomb was discovered in 1604, and 'new stars' seen that year were connected with the changes heralded by the Rosicrucian manifestos.[25]

Within the many strange forms and diagrams of the *Nao-*

metria, there is one described by Yates as 'a crudely shaped rose design, with a cross in the centre'. (See Plate 18.) A.E. Waite believed it to be the 'first example of Rosicrucian rose and cross symbolism', to which Yates responds fairly: 'I cannot say I am altogether convinced.'[25]

The design is full of the *Naometria's* strange combinations of dates, and it might easily be argued it is not a rose at all. If we do see it as rose-like, it is an eight-petalled rose, not found in nature, but found in the design Maier sent to James. The 'petals' in the two diagrams could even be said to have the same shape. I am not, of course, in any position to state that Maier knew the design in the *Naometria*; or, even if he did, that he was attempting to refer to it. But there is nevertheless a connection between the two images, independent of their forms. They are both closely linked to King James, through their contexts. And they have both aroused the almost identical question: 'Is it a Rosicrucian symbol or isn't it?' A question which is perfectly fitting for King James.

My enquiries into the alchemical library of George Erskine (pages 99–103) also show that James, in all likelihood, was a recipient both of the Rosicrucian manifestos, the *Fama* and the *Confessio,* and of Schweighardt's Rosicrucian writings and images.

4. Sacred architecture: Stonehenge and the Globe Theatre

Stonehenge

In the final chapter of *The Theatre of the World,* Frances Yates describes the remarkable 'mistake' made by Inigo Jones regarding the origin of Stonehenge. Jones researched Stonehenge and declared, quite falsely, that it was a Roman Temple. The type of Roman Temple which Jones declared it to be, which he had discovered in the writings of Vitruvius, had, furthermore, not in fact been a temple at all, but a *theatre*. (Frances Yates considers it impossible that Jones would not have known this.) Jones concludes his argument about Stonehenge by comparing it with Solomon's Temple:

> Yea further, (if lawful to compare an idolatrous place with so divine a Work) was not the Temple at Hierusalem adorned with the figures of Cherubims, that thereby the Nations of the Earth might know it was the Habitation of the living God? And why not in like Manner this Temple...?

All this is described in a book called *The Most Notable Antiquity of Great Britain, Called Stone-Heng, on Salisbury Plain, Restored,* published 3 years after Inigo Jones's death by his son-in-law, John Webb. The whole book, says Yates, was either: 'really by Jones, or closely based on manuscript notes by him'.

Of particular interest to our theme is Jones's description of how it was none other than King James, characteristically,[26] who initiated this research into Stonehenge:

> King James, in his Progress, the year One thousand six hundred and twenty, being at Wilton, and discoursing of this Antiquity [Stonehenge], I was sent for by the Right Honourable William, then Earl of Pembroke, *and received there his Majesty's Commands to produce,* out of mine own Practice in Architecture, and Experience in Antiquities Abroad, *what possibly I could discover concerning this of Stone-Heng.*[27] (My emphases.)

The Globe Theatre

Yates goes on to say that although James's comments on Vitruvius's Roman Theatre (Temple) are untrue in relation to the origins of Stonehenge, they have, in her opinion, a great deal of truth in relation to the origins of the Globe Theatre. (Much of the rest of her book sets out to substantiate this claim.)

As Inigo Jones clearly knew that Vitruvius was referring to a theatre, and as Jones had first-hand experience of the Globe Theatre, Yates claims that although Jones is not normally believed to have concerned himself with public theatres, such as the Globe, his remarks on Stonehenge may prove otherwise. Jones's interpretation of Stonehenge, says Yates, may tell us that he saw a theatre like the Globe as: 'A theatre merged with a temple, or a temple merged with a theatre, or a temple-theatre behind which loomed the Temple at Jerusalem.'[28]

Because Yates never chose to focus on the influence of King James, she fails to connect James's part in initiating the research about Stonehenge with what she reveals elsewhere about James's links with the Globe Theatre.

In her earlier book, *The Art of Memory*, Yates is clearly of the opinion that Fludd knew of a side to James that was hidden from public view.[29] This is nowhere more fully stated than in relation to Shakespeare's Globe Theatre. Yates's view is that the source of all that lies behind the Globe Theatre is to be found in Robert Fludd's 'Theatre Memory System'. This 'theatre memory system' is described in Fludd's *Utriusque Cosmi ... Historia*. And thus Yates, writing in the 1960s, can ground-breakingly declare: 'We have been able to excavate the Globe Theatre from its hiding place in *Utriusque Cosmi ... Historia* [where] it has been well and truly hidden [...] for three and a half centuries.' *Utriusque Cosmi ... Historia*, of course, was the book so loftily dedicated to King James. Yates asks therefore: 'Is Fludd's system of the twenty-four memory theatres in the zodiac [...] deliberately contrived to conceal his allusion to the Globe Theatre from all but the initiated, of whom we must suppose that James I was one?'[30]

Yates also tells us that 'James I contributed a considerable amount towards the cost of the rebuilding' of the Globe, after it burned down in 1613.[31] Fludd says he had a 'real' public theatre in mind when describing his 'theatre memory system', depicted by him in his engraving 'Theatrum Orbi'. Yates argues this must surely have been the Globe, it being the most famous of the London public theatres, and having such a similar name—Orbi/World/Globe. Yates asks, since Part One of *Utriusque Cosmi ... Historia* had been dedicated to King James,

> ... would it not have been a good way of keeping up that monarch's interest in the second volume to allude in the memory system to the newly rebuilt Globe, towards the erection of which James had largely contributed and which was the theatre of his own company of players, the King's men?[32]

5. *Alchemical library*

Adrian Gilbert tells us that, despite James I's fear of 'anything that [...] smelled of magic', 'he was very interested in alchemy and possessed a considerable library on the subject'.[33]

I do not know where he gleaned this information, as I have not found any reference to a library on alchemy owned by King James. However, the two significant alchemical libraries in Britain dating from the beginning of the 17th Century, bear many of the telltale signs of a link with King James.

The first of these libraries belonged to Sir Robert Ker, or Carr, first Earl of Ancrum (1578–1654). It includes works by Hermes, Sendivogius, Basil Valentine, Robert Fludd and

Michael Maier, for example Maier's *The lawes of the Rosie Cross*. It also includes a copy of Schweighardt's accessibly-titled Rosicrucian work: *Speculum Sophicum Rhodostauroticum*.

As Adam McClean says, the library unquestionably 'reveals his [Ker's] deep interest in Hermetic and Rosicrucian material'.

But who was Robert Carr?

He was the cousin of his more famous namesake, Robert Carr, Earl of Somerset, the first of King James's close 'favourites'. Both Robert Carrs came to England with King James in 1603. Robert Carr, Earl of Somerset's links to King James, and his spectacular rise and fall, are well documented. Far less is known of Robert Carr, Earl of Ancrum. They have even at times been assumed to be the same person, for example in relation to John Donne, a close friend of Ker, Earl of Ancrum. But what is known about him reveals a continued connection with King James. He was knighted in 1605 or 1606. He was once directly pardoned by the King, having killed in a duel one Charles Maxwell, who had apparently challenged Carr, in order to please the Duke of Buckingham (James's *second* favourite). Carr also worked closely both for Prince Henry and for Prince (later King) Charles.[34]

It is the second collection, though, that begs the questions.

It belonged to Sir George Erskine (*c.*1570–1646) and consists of 'an important collection of alchemical manuscripts, including a rare and unusual alchemical document, the *Ripley Scroll*.[35] This description does not give an adequate sense of the massive scale and importance of this collection. There are seven items in all—six large volumes of transcriptions of Hermetic texts and the *Ripley Scroll*. The five volumes that survive total 'over 1500 folios with transcriptions of about 140 texts'. Volume Four contains very early translations of the *Fama Fraternitatis* and the *Confessio Fraternitatis* into Scots

English. The titles of the remaining volumes read like a pantheon of the alchemical and the arcane—Hermes Trismegistos, Raymond Lull, Arnold de Villa Nova, Roger Bacon, Pico della Mirandola, Agrippa, Theophilus Schweighardt, Basil Valentine, to name but the most well-known. Most of them are in Latin, e.g: 'Alchemical recipes in Latin, with pen drawings of distillation apparatus and pulley wheels.'[36] The *Ripley Scroll* is 'a parchment roll 18 feet long and 3 feet wide which purports to set out the steps necessary for the attainment of the Philosopher's Stone', by the 15th century Canon of Bridlington, George Ripley.

Sir George Erskine's grandson, Lord Cromertie, described Erskine as: 'A great student in natural philosophy, even to a considerable advancement in the Hermetick schoole,' saying that he 'had a correspondence in very remote parts with the sonnes of Hermes'.

According to Cromertie, much of the collection was sent to Erskine by the 'Society at Hess' through one 'Dr Politius'.[37] Politius said that, 'by direction of that society [his] chief errand to Scotland was to confer with him [Erskine].'

But no one has been able to explain Sir George Erskine's interest in these matters, given all that is known about him. Ian McCallum writes: 'It is difficult to reconcile Erskine's very practical and mundane activities [...] with his involvement in alchemy and Rosicrucianism.'[35]

And again:

It is remarkable that so little is recorded about Erskine's alchemical interests. In such a well-known family with very extensive aristocratic and royal court connections he was perhaps not so outstanding, but he was nevertheless an eminent figure of his time. He has been described as the most important of a number of followers of hermetic philosophy or alchemy in the time of King James VI, but apart from his manuscripts it is not known to what extent he was involved in practical alchemy.

What we *do* know about George Erskine is that he was from boyhood a friend of James VI (I). They had been fellow-pupils under the royal tutor George Buchanan. James refers to him in a letter, ordering that lands be given to him, as '... our trustie and welbeloved Sir George Erskine of Innerteill'. In 1618 James made him a member of the 'Secret or Privy Council' in Scotland, saying that he, James, has '... perfectly understood the sufficiency and qualification of Sir George Erskine and his good affection to the advancement of all things which may concern our service'.

In view of their link going back to boyhood, and in the light of all else we know about King James, it seems barely credible that James would not have known of Erskine's vast esoteric collection. We are surely entitled to speculate, even, that James was closely linked with all that lay behind this collection. Everything else in the present book has shown that it was not James's way to carry things out himself, directly. Apart from all we have said about Bacon and Shakespeare, we have seen this in the case of William Schaw regarding Freemasonry, Inigo Jones regarding Stonehenge, and with regard to the translation of the Bible. To say that James 'delegated' is a vast understatement. We should also remember that the full title of the *Confessio* translated into Scots in Erskine's collection, is: 'The Confession of the Laudable fraternitie of the most honored ordour of the Rosy Cross *wrettin to the learned of Europe*.' (My emphasis.)

Whatever else people may have denied James, no one has ever doubted his status as one of the 'learned of Europe', and therefore as one of those to whom the manifesto was addressed. Dr Politius's 'errand to Scotland' might make a great deal more sense in this light. I could easily imagine that a considerable part of Erskine's collection was in fact transcribed and translated with James in mind, if not at his behest.

One last typically Jamesian detail attests to this thought. Lord Cromertie gave Erskine's collection into public hands, to the Royal College of Physicians in Edinburgh, on 19 June 1707. 1707 was the year when James's long-cherished ideal finally took place, the *union* of Scotland and England. 19 June was King James's birthday. This vast esoteric library, by whatever means this came about, is nothing less than King James's birthday present!

Cromertie inscribed on the first page of the first volume: 'Affectionately and humbly offdred on the nyneteen of June An Chr 1707.' He states it again in Latin on the seventh item, where, with its sequence of sevens, its mystic symbols, and its reference to Erskine's membership of James's 'secret council', it reads, whether or not it was intended this way, like some kind of alchemical seal on this connection:

> Edinburgi, decimo nono di Junii anno millesimo septingenterimo et septimo, hoc misticum symbole in avita bibliotheca Doni Georgii Areskine [...] philosophiae hermeticae et allummus et decor, Regumque sui aevi a Conciliis Secretis...

Ker and Erskine, owners of the two most significant esoteric libraries in Britain in James's time, were not only both known personally to King James, but also had links with each other. Adam McClean tells us that watermarks disclose that they both used the same paper, in particular in the case of the Rosicrucian manifestos.[38] In this crucial instance, then, these two libraries show they share a common source.

Adam McClean comments on this:

Through the discovery of the links between these manuscripts we can trace a thread running through a number of
aristocrats, primarily of Scottish origin, close to King
Charles I and King James, back to Robert Ker. It is not
impossible that further research into these personalities
and their circle of friends might uncover more documentary evidence of the unfolding of Rosicrucianism in
Britain.

I would suggest that a crucial link in all this, who has hardly
ever yet been considered, being, as in the best detective
stories, the very last person to be suspected, is King James
himself. I am less certain, however, that his activity will be
found detailed in any 'documentary evidence'.

6. *Shakespeare's circle*

There are several purely biographical links between King
James and Shakespeare to which little attention has so far
been paid.

In 1603, when James came to London, Shakespeare found
favour with the King extraordinarily quickly. This was also
true of Bacon, who was knighted within four months of
James's arrival; but with Shakespeare it was even more dramatic: 'Within ten days of arriving in London, although
besieged by other claims for his attention, the new King took
the Lord Chamberlain's troupe under his own royal patronage. Shakespeare was now one of the King's men.'[39]

Alvin Kernan describes this in more detail:

Soon after James arrived in London the Crown issued a
warrant to the company of players for which William
Shakespeare was the resident playwright and part owner.

The business went through the red tape of the court bureaucracy in the extraordinarily short time of two days, and was completed by 17th May. The King's Men obviously had some good friend near the throne, perhaps the earl of Southampton, perhaps the earl of Pembroke, probably both.' (My emphasis.)

Henry Wriothesley, Earl of Southampton

These latter two individuals are of enormous importance in Shakespeare's life, and rightly appear in all discussions concerning the authorship of his works. Shakespeare dedicated both *Venus and Adonis* and *The Rape of Lucrece* to Henry Wriothesley, Earl of Southampton, saying in the dedication to the latter: 'The love I dedicate to your lordship is without end, [...] what I have done is yours; what I have to do is yours.'

The only other named dedicatees of Shakespeare's work are the two brothers William Herbert (Earl of Pembroke) and Philip Herbert (Earl of Montgomery) to whom the *First Folio* is addressed, though it was published seven years after Shakespeare's death, in 1623.

Heminges and Condell, who edited the First Folio, speak in their dedication to the Herbert brothers—the 'Incomparable Pair of Brethren'—of the connection they had with Shakespeare during his life:

Since your lordships have been pleased to think these trifles something heretofore, and have prosecuted both them and their author, living, with so much favour, we hope that, they outliving him, and he not having the fate, common with some, to be executor to his own writings, you will use the like indulgence toward them you have done unto their parent.[40]

Both Southampton and the Earl of Pembroke, moreover, had known Shakespeare since the very beginning of his writing career. *Venus and Adonis,* published in 1593, when he was 28, is described by Shakespeare as 'the first heir of my invention', and the title page of *Titus Adronicus* (1594), often perceived as Shakespeare's earliest play, tells us that it had been performed by the 'Earl of Pembroke's Men'.

(The only other dedication by Shakespeare is of the Sonnets: 'To the only begetter of these ensuing sonnets. Mr. W. H.' The obvious candidates for this are generally imagined to be either William Herbert or Henry Wriothesley.)

The 'Essex Rebellion' of 1601, in which Southampton played a major role, has often been mentioned in discussions about the authorship.[41] This is particularly because on the eve of the rebellion, at the request of Essex's party, Shakespeare's company performed *Richard II,* where the reigning monarch is deposed. This led to Queen Elizabeth's famous response: 'Know you not that I am Richard the Second?'

What has been paid almost no attention when discussing this in relation to the authorship of Shakespeare, is that the purpose of the Essex rebellion was to try and bring King James to the throne:

> A Stuart party led by the earl of Essex was pushing James as the successor the queen [Elizabeth] stubbornly refused to name. In 1601, desperate at the loss of favor and income, Essex launched an abortive rebellion. His chief lieutenant was the earl of Southampton, who was also Shakespeare's patron.[42]

As Kernan points out, therefore, more than two years before Elizabeth's death and James's accession, Shakespeare's patron, Southampton, was already seen in the most favourable of lights by Shakespeare's royal patron-to-be, King James. James ordered the release of Southampton and the other surviving conspirators (Essex had been executed) soon after crossing the border. This leads Kernan to speculate whether this may not have been the reason for Shakespeare's so speedy preferral:

> Shakespeare's company may have been given the royal nod because they were the theatrical best, but they also had at least a modest personal claim on the king and his government. [...] Shakespeare and his company appear to have shared in the royal gratitude for support in a critical time.[43]

In the light of the present book, the performance of *Richard II* in connection with the Essex rebellion is important because it shows that in at least one instance a direct external connection can be seen between the impulse borne by James VI & I and Shakespeare's History Plays, written before 1603.

'The Incomparable Pair of Brethren'

William Herbert, Earl of Pembroke, is mentioned on the title page of Shakespeare's first play, *Titus Andronicus*, in 1594, and the First Folio is later dedicated to him and his brother in 1623. He therefore has a connection with Shakespeare's work from its very beginning to its full publication after Shakespeare's death.

King James's connection to both William and Philip Herbert was not only *far* more extensive than that to the Earl of Southampton, but also far more intimate. As Kernan says, regarding the likelihood that it was William, Earl of Pembroke, who had preferred Shakespeare to the King:

> Pembroke, a handsome young man, caught James's eye at once. By the time of the coronation in July [1603] he was familiar enough with the king to be able to get away with kissing him on the lips rather than the hand at the cere-

mony, and *he had great influence with the king from the earliest days of the reign.* (My emphasis.)[44]

A Venetian (Giovanni Scaramelli) present at the ceremony is the source of this anecdote: 'The Earl of Pembroke, a handsome youth, who is always with the king and always joking with him, actually kissed his Majesty's face, whereupon the king laughed and gave him a little cuff.'[45]

James soon developed affection also for Pembroke's younger brother, 'the even more handsome Philip, who as a result of his intimacy was made earl of Montgomery in 1605.'[46] When Philip Herbert married, James showed the kind of behaviour which has led, hardly surprisingly, to his being described as 'an intolerable fellow'. Philip Herbert and his new bride slept on their wedding night in the 'council chamber'—'where the king gave them in the morning before they were up a *reveille-matin* in his shirt and nightgown and spent a good hour with them in the bed or upon, choose which you will believe best.'[47]

One famous anecdote even brings King James, the Herbert brothers and William Shakespeare together. The King spent much of the autumn of 1603 at Wilton House, near Salisbury, home of the Countess of Pembroke, Mary Sidney, sister of Sir Philip Sidney and mother of William and Philip Herbert. The King's Men were paid the unusually large sum for the time of £30 to come and perform a play at Wilton before the King. Mary Sidney wrote to her son William in a letter (now lost, but well attested to) telling him to come to Wilton, to see *As You Like It,* saying: 'We have the man Shakespeare with us.'[48]

Frances Yates tells us that King James 'frequently visited the Herbert seat of Wilton'. Inigo Jones, we remember, recounts being called for by William Herbert in 1620 to come and meet the King at Wilton, to discuss Stonehenge.

King James's links with the Herbert (Sidney) family in fact go back much further than 1603, through the profound admiration he and Sir Philip Sidney held for each other. In his *Apology for Poetry*, Sidney had spoken of: 'Sweet poesy, that hath anciently had kings, emperors [...] not only to favour poets, but to be poets', and he cites 'King James of Scotland' as one of the examples of this in his own time. (He also praises James's tutor George Buchanan: 'The tragedies of Buchanan do justly bring forth a divine admiration.') Sidney had a close connection to James's favourite, Patrick, Master of Gray. In his last letter to Gray, in 1586, a few months before his death, Sidney wrote: 'And which is the last, or rather the first point, hold me, I beseech you, in the gracious remembrance of your King, whom indeed I love.' When Sidney died James wrote two elegies for him, one of them a sonnet, which he also translated into Latin.

The King's playwright

Although popular opinion always likes to think of Shakespeare's connection with Queen Elizabeth, people have begun to notice that incomparably more plays were performed before King James than ever were before Elizabeth I. In Anthony Holden's biography of Shakespeare we read:

> In the thirteen years between the King's accession and the poet's death, the King's men would play at court no fewer than 187 times—an average of thirteen royal command performances a year compared with three during Elizabeth's reign. He [James] paid twice as much, what's more ... [49]

It is this hugely increased *court connection* of Shakespeare's, and the way this is directly reflected in Shakespeare's work, which is the subject of Kernan's book. There is nowhere better to study the extent of James's relation to Shakespeare specifically as *patron*. In his introduction, Kernan writes:

> Our democratic age will resist even a partial transformation of Shakespeare into a courtly servant and a recipient of patronage. But in the palace Shakespeare, whose roots still lay in the public theater, like those of many another European court playwright in the Renaissance, takes a place among the age's great patronage playwrights [...] In the court setting, Shakespeare's great succession of Stuart plays [...] becomes one of the master oeuvres of European patronage art.[50]

An aspect to these court performances which is even more alien to modern minds is their at least occasional calendrical significance. *King Lear*, for example, was performed before King James on St Stephen's night, 1606. The only play that James specifically asked to see twice was *The Merchant of Venice*. It was performed first on Shrove Sunday, 1605. James commanded a second performance 3 days later, on Shrove Tuesday. Steve Sohmer, for one, has described this to be because the opening scenes of the play are 'set on Shrove Tuesday and include episodes of Shrovetide masquing'. Sohmer, who has written extensively on this subject, comments: 'This gesture reveals an aspect of James's personality which was certainly familiar to his court: *the king was a calendrical man*.'[51] (My emphasis)

Sohmer shows evidence for this in James's connections with George Buchanan and Tycho Brahe, and in his reforming of the Scottish calendar in 1599. But the remark 'the king was a calendrical man' may also strike us in connection with some of the strange dating 'coincidences' we have found in relation to King James.

It is also of note that despite all the material in Shakespeare which might be seen as seditious, and despite all the censorship and banning of plays, Shakespeare went, at all times, 'Scot-free': 'In the 577 cases of *Scandalum Magnatum* prosecuted in Star Chamber during James's reign, William Shakespeare's name nowhere appears.'[52]

7. *Seven anecdotes about King James*

More work in an hour

> He loved loose freedoms and gross pleasures, yet he never lost himself in them. He loved arguments and theological hair-splitting, yet he had at any moment that sense of actuality which is rare in such theoretical minds. He loved idleness and pleasure; but when he was rebuked for it he answered by saying that he did more work in an hour than others in a day, but his body was too weak to work without interruption. He added that he was like a Spanish jennet which could run one course well but could not hold out. In every single spasm of labour he 'could listen to one man, talk to another, and observe a third. Sometimes he could do five things at once.'[53]

Reconciling opposites

A typically Geminian, Solomonic act of making peace between opposites, or warring factions, was the Feast of Peace James held when he was 21. It may resound for us, if we let it, with the tying at the metaphorical wrist of Bacon and Shakespeare.

> He prepared for himself, in that auspicious year, a feast of peace [...] The great houses of Scotland were divided and

ravaged by bitter feuds. The King determined to end all that. He gathered all the hostile lords at Holyrood [...] banqueted them [...] and then [...] caused a procession to be formed, *two by two, each one of each pious or scornful or bewildered pair handfasted to his worst enemy*. The King came down and took his place at their head. Out from the palace the procession went, up the High Street of Edinburgh, between the heads of gazing citizens, up to the market cross. There [...] a table had been spread 'even in the midst, among their enemies'. Public proclamation of concord was made; foes drank to each other, and the King to all.[54] (My emphasis.)

'His breeks in his hand'

One of the many assaults on James's person offers us a bizarre glimpse of the King caught with his trousers down, emerging from the lavatory, in mortal danger. The raid on Holyrood House, orchestrated primarily by James's cousin, Francis Stewart Earl of Bothwell and Countess Atholl had been rigorously and successfully prepared through the night of 23 July, 1593.

> At eight o'clock in the morning everything had gone without a hitch. When the raiders, pistol in hand, tiptoed up to the King's rooms, they experienced a further piece of luck [...] James had just risen from his bed and, before dressing, had retired to 'his secret place'. It was in his nightgown, therefore, that the monarch appeared, and with 'his breeks in his hand'. [...] There stood before him, sword in one hand, pistol in the other, the man he most disliked and dreaded in the world ...[55]

(The latter was a justifiable assertion given that at the witchcraft trials of 1590 James had learned how a waxen image, wrapped in royal cloth had been passed round from person to person, each one declaring: 'This is King James the Sixth, ordained to be consumed at the instance of a noble man, Francis Earl of Bothwell.')

> There was nothing for it but to put as brave a face on the matter as he could, and hope for the best. 'Francis,' he cried, 'thou will do me no ill will?' 'Lo, my good bairn,' was Francis's answer (according to his own account), 'ye that have given out that I sought your life [...] see [...] it is now in this hand.'

James's reply to this, standing there 'breeks in hand', was, according to one version: 'What do ye seek? Do ye seek my soul? Ye shall not have my soul. Strike if ye dare, false traitors.'[56]

'Be absolute for death'

An event from the winter of 1603 must have revealed to all who heard report of it—as it does to us now—the real *strangeness*, by ordinary mortally-minded standards, of the new monarch. A plot had been uncovered whose intention was to seize the king, in order either to replace him, or to force him to grant religious concessions. At Westminster, on a December morning, three of the conspirators, Markham, Grey and Cobham, were to be brought out one by one to the public scaffold to be beheaded. It was, we are told, 'a dark and rainy day'. Markham, having prepared himself as best he could, was told he was too 'ill prepared' to die, and was therefore taken back inside to meditate two hours further. Grey was brought out, but when, after lengthy preparations, he turned towards the executioner, was told that Cobham was in fact to die first, and so was also taken back inside. Cobham was brought out, said prayers and made a short speech, only to be told that he was to meet, one more time, his fellow-conspirators. Markham and Grey were brought back, mounted the scaffold, and the three conspirators gazed at each other, in the words of the time, 'like men beheaded and met in the other world'. Their crimes were read out again, they accepted their guilt and the justness of their punishment, at which moment they were told they had been pardoned by the King. They would still be imprisoned, but were not to die. There was 'wild cheering' from the crowd, and then, in Charles Williams's words: 'The prisoners were removed again to prison, and the horrible display of mercy was done.'

Williams adds: 'It was the King's plan; no other would have dared it, and hardly any other could have managed it.'[57] The story has rightly been seen as a source for the equally strange behaviour of Duke Vincentio in Shakespeare's *Measure For Measure*. Vincentio makes almost every major character believe at some point in the play that they are about to die. Only when they have accepted this, is their life given back to them. Horrendous as this experience may appear, acted out in public by the scaffold, it was turned by John Donne into his regular spiritual practice.

Three deaths

It is surprising that no one appears to have commented on the completely opposite ways in which Bacon and Shakespeare are said to have met their deaths. Put simply, Bacon died of cold and Shakespeare of heat (a fever.) This is how Joseph Devey retells the often told story of Bacon's fatal experiment with refrigeration:

> It struck him, when examining the subject of antiseptics, that snow might preserve flesh from corruption, and he resolved to try the experiment. One frosty morning [...] he

alighted at Highgate, and proceeded to stuff a fowl which he bought at a neighbouring cottage, with snow that he gathered from the ground. At the end of the operation he felt in his limbs a sudden chill, and was obliged to retire to the earl of Arundel's house hard by [...] A week later, on Easter Sunday, 1626, he died.[58]

Shakespeare's demise was rather less scientific in origin. According to popular report, soon after Easter, in 1616: 'Shakespear, Drayton and Ben Jonson, had a merry meeting, and it seems drank too hard, for Shakespear died of a feavour there contracted.'[59]

King James had had experience of both kinds of experiment. In King James's service was a Dutch scientist Cornelis Drebbel (1572–1633.) In his laboratory (at Eltham) he experimented, among other things, with weather phenomena and artificial incubation. (A visitor said that Drebbel 'could make it rain, lighten and thunder [...] as if it had come about naturally from heaven' and that he could hatch eggs 'without any Ducks or Chickens by [...] even in midwinter'.) In 1620 he exhibited before King James a submarine, which disappeared under the Thames for three hours, holding, according to the Dutch scientist, Huygens, who witnessed it, 'the King, his court, and several thousand Londoners in excited expectation'.

Another of Drebbel's experiments has a direct connection with Bacon's refrigeration attempts, and Bacon almost certainly refers to it in *De Augmentis*, when he mentions 'the late experiment of artificial freezing'. Brian Vickers, in his notes to Bacon's *New Atlantis*, tells us:

He [Drebbel] gave a demonstration of instruments he had invented to chill the air before King James in the Great Hall of Westminster, making it 'so cold on a summer's day that the King and his nobles and many great lords were forced to flee.[60]

There are several descriptions of James and his court enjoying experiments of the kind which supposedly led to Shakespeare's death.

Sir John Harington, 'himself far from prudish', wrote to a friend in shock at the partying that accompanied the visit to Britain of the King of Denmark:

> The sports began each day in such manner and such sorte, as well nigh persuaded me of Mahomet's paradise. We had women, and indeed wine too, of such plenty as would have astonished each sober beholder. Our feasts were magnificent, and the two royal guests did most lovingly embrace each other at table. I think the Dane hath strangely wrought on our good English nobles; for those, whom I never could get to taste good liquor, now follow the fashion, and wallow in beastly delights. The ladies abandon their sobriety, and are seen to roll about in intoxication.[61]

Harington also described one 'great feast', during this visit, where 'the representation of Solomon his Temple and the coming of the queen of Sheba was made, or (as I may better say) was meant to have been made, before their Majesties.'

As an alternative picture of King Solomon and the Queen of Sheba at the court of King James it is worth quoting at some length:

> The Lady who did play the Queen [of Sheba's] part, did carry most precious gifts to both their majesties; but forgetting the steppes arising to the canopy, overset her caskets into his Danish Majestie's lap, and fell at his feet, tho I rather think it was in his face [...] His Majesty [of Denmark] then got up and would dance with the Queen of

Sheba; but he fell down and humbled himself before her, and was carried to an inner chamber, and laid on a bed of state; which was not a little defiled with the presents of the Queen which had been bestowed on his garments; such as wine, cream, jelly, beverage, cakes, spices, and other good matters. The entertainment and show went forward, and most of the presenters went backward, or fell down; wine did so occupy their upper chambers. Now did appear in rich dress, Hope, Faith, and Charity. Hope did assay to speak, but wine rendered her endeavours so feeble that she withdrew, and hoped the King would excuse her brevity: Faith was then all alone, for I am certain she was not joyned with good works, and left the court in a staggering condition: Charity came to the King's feet; and seemed to cover the multitude of sins her sisters had committed [...] She then returned to Hope and Faith, who were both sick and spewing in the lower hall.[62]

King Solamona, in Bacon's *New Atlantis*, is described as having a 'large heart, inscrutable for good'. Bacon, of course, is referring to the Biblical King Solomon's 'largeness of heart'. When King James died, in 1625, and a post-mortem was done, the physicians found, as James might have wished: 'his heart of an extraordinary bigness, all his vitals sound, as also his head, which was very full of brains; but his blood was wonderfully tainted with melancholy; and the corruption thereof supposed the cause of his death.'[63]

Chapter Seven

SHAKESPEARE—THE CHIEF MUSICIAN

Psalm 46: a curious coincidence?

At the very beginning of his book *Who Wrote Shakespeare?* John Michell refers to the 'curious coincidence' of Psalm 46, as translated in the King James Bible. To conclude this present book we will also broach this great unsolved riddle of the Shakespearian authorship debate.

The coincidence is as follows: in the 46th Psalm the 46th word from the beginning is 'shake' and the 46th word from the end is 'speare'.[1] (This is only true of the translation of the Psalm in the King James Bible, see plate 19).

John Michell writes about this:

> Either it is an amazing freak of chance, or it imputes great cunning and daring to someone of high position in the time of King James, someone who oversaw the compilation of the Authorized Version of the English Bible and was also aware of a mystery about the works of Shakespeare.

If it isn't an 'amazing freak of chance', in my own opinion by *far* the most likely candidate for this is King James himself.

No one, presumably, would dispute that he was 'someone of high position in the time of King James', nor that he was 'someone who oversaw the compilation of the Authorized Version of the English Bible'. Michell himself describes the process the translation went through. It was carried out first by 'a committee of the most learned clerical scholars in the kingdom [...] Their work was submitted for approval to the bishops and leading theologians, then to the Privy Council and *finally to the King himself.*' (My emphasis.)

Regarding the remark that whoever was behind this numerical act was 'aware of a mystery about the works of Shakespeare', we should first look at what else can be found hidden in or around this Psalm.

Michell notes that the King James Bible was finished in 1610, when Shakespeare himself was 46. It was not published until 1611, when Shakespeare was 47 and King James 45. I am not certain this is the main significance, though, of the number 46. 46 is twice 23—and 23 was an important number for both King James and Shakespeare.

Shakespeare was born and died on 23 April, St George's Day. Shakespeare's First Folio was published in 1623. We also find references to the number in the plays. For example, Hamlet had last seen Yorick, whose skull he finds, 23 years previously. Cymbeline's two sons are 22 and 23. King James VI (I) set sail for Denmark, to meet his bride, when he was 23, on the night of 22 October 1589. He was married on 23 November. He met Tycho Brahe on 20.3.1590. When James was 46 his son Prince Henry died, and the second hugely important marriage in his life took place, that between his daughter, Princess Elizabeth, and Frederick, Elector Palatine.[2] The importance of Psalm 46 as 2 × 23 is also made likely by the pre-eminence of Psalm 23: 'The Lord is my shepherd; I shall not want'.

Shakespeare's name also appears *twice* in the Psalm—or in two halves—*and so does King James's*. Psalm 46 is the only Psalm in the first 100 where the name *Jacob* (James) appears *twice*. (The only other ones, by my reckoning, are Psalms 114 and 132.) Furthermore, we have seen already ('The King was a calendrical man') that James was no stranger at all to things numerical.

A letter of King James's to Robert Cecil reveals both his concern with number and his conscious connecting of himself with the Biblical Jacob:

> I may justly say that the name James included a prophetical mystery of my fortune, for as a Jacob I wrestled with my arms upon the 5 August for my life, and overcame; upon the 5 November I wrestled and overcame with my wit ...[3]

Not only this, but Psalm 46 is one of a group of Psalms addressed to King David's 'chief musician'. Psalm 45's opening words on the relationship of the chief court poet to the King must surely have appealed to King James:

> My heart is stirred by a noble theme,
> in a King's honour I utter the song I have made,
> and my tongue runs like the pen of an expert scribe.[4]

Nor was this the only time that a book of King James's would place Shakespeare and James in such close proximity. The verse accompanying James's image, on the frontispiece of his *Works* (1616), has always been attributed to Shakespeare. (See Plate 15)

Let us return then to address Michell's final criterion that the person responsible for the insertion into the 46th Psalm 'was also aware of a mystery about the works of Shakespeare'.

If we see James himself as the one who inserted 'shakespeare' into Psalm 46, the message becomes *not*, as many have speculated, that Shakespeare, or Shakespeare-alias-Bacon, translated the King James Bible. This is anyway not a message that can be read into the insertion of the name. The message becomes, as so much else points to, both within the Psalm and elsewhere, that Shakespeare is to be recognized as James/Jacob's 'chief musician', that they speak, as it were, with the same voice.

The importance of Psalm 46 would then become that it contains James's own personal acknowledgement of this most remarkable 'mystery about the works of Shakespeare'.

End and beginning

By way of conclusion, I shall briefly summarize the journey we have made.

I looked first at the importance of Shakespeare's life as an actor for any discussion of the authorship of his plays. I then looked at some of the little-known remarks of Rudolf Steiner, who states that William Shakespeare and Francis Bacon were both inspired by the same individual. Should this be the case, it would obviously shed fascinating light on the true connection between Shakespeare and Bacon.

Oddly, though Steiner made his remarks some 80 years ago, no one during that time had correctly identified—within the English-speaking world—the exact individual Steiner was seeing as standing behind these two great geniuses of artistic and scientific life in Britain. When I looked closely at Steiner's remarks it became clear, though very surprising, whom he was referring to. I then found, almost more surprisingly, that startling evidence for Steiner's claim is to be found within the lives and the works of Bacon and Shakespeare.

Having explored the difference of this perspective from that which states that Bacon was the author of Shakespeare's works, I turned my attention to the strange contradictory figure of James I, and to why he came to be referred to as 'Great Britain's Solomon'.

I then re-examined, in the fresh light of these discoveries, what history and historical anecdote have to say about King James. I chose not to discuss the many differing viewpoints held by historians and biographers about King James—whether negative or positive—in the attempt to gain a new perspective. Concealed within the history books, I discovered not only the most thoroughgoing personal connections with Bacon and Shakespeare, but many other remarkable connections, including, for example, a deep involvement in all that lay behind the Globe Theatre.

Finally, along this route, I even stumbled across an answer to the fascinating authorship riddle of Psalm 46—an answer which completely satisfies all the necessary criteria given by John Michell in *Who Wrote Shakespeare?* Readers must obviously make up their own minds here, but Psalm 46 may very well be the nearest we are likely to get to a written statement by King James himself, regarding the mystery of the authorship of Shakespeare.

The Globe Theatre, presumably unintentionally, also gave somewhat uncanny expression to this mystery, in an education brochure of 2003—the 400th anniversary of James 1's accession to the English throne. (See plate 20. I am grateful to Shakespeare's Globe for their permission to reproduce this.)

This small book does, then, offer answers to some rather big questions. These answers, of course, only open the way to new grounds for questioning and experience. I hope the book may also be looked on, therefore, as a beginning.

NOTES

Introduction

1 John Michell: *Who Wrote Shakespeare?*, praised on its cover as: 'The best overview yet of the authorship controversy.'

2 Ibid. p. 257.

3 p. 261.

4 A highly developed individual who has developed faculties of spiritual perception (Ed.).

5 Friedrich Hiebel has written on this question in German, in a book no longer in print, *Das Drama des Dramas.*

Chapter 1

1 John Southworth, *Shakespeare The Player, A Life in Theatre.* (For publisher and date, as with all further books mentioned, see Bibliography.)

2 Ibid. pp. 10–11.

3 Ibid. p. 10.

4 Ibid. pp. 278–279.

5 Harley Granville-Barker: *Prefaces to Shakespeare, Vol. VI*, pp. 166 & 165.

6 Printed in *The Anthroposophical Quarterly*, Christmas 1928.

7 This and the following two quotations from: 'Notes of a Lecture by Rudolf Steiner at the Workman's School in Berlin, 1902,' *Anthroposophical News Sheet*, Vol. 13, 9–10 Jan. 1935.

8 Ibid.

Twenty years later, in 1922, in Stratford-upon-Avon, on Shakespeare's birthday, 23 April, Rudolf Steiner describes the extraordinary spiritual consequences of Shakespeare's creative activity. Shakespeare's characters, says Steiner, are not mere imitations of life, or the result of intellectual ideas, but are created specifically for the stage. Shakespeare's aim was none other than to create, in the world of the theatre, *living* characters. And because he was so successful in this, if through spiritual vision one can transfer one's experience of these characters into the spiritual worlds, one discovers that they continue to live there. This is not at all the case, says Steiner, with lesser dramatists. He continues (in his report of his lecture tour in Holland and England in 1922, *Anthroposophic News Sheet,* 24 February 1935): 'Shakespeare is a theatre-realist, he creates for the stage... He knew that it is not possible to produce characters on the stage, which are imitated from life... Shakespeare is not an imitator of life. Shakespeare is a creative spirit who works with the material that lies before him. In this way he created his living characters, that enable us to look into the astral plane, into Devachan and into the whole spiritual world. There, these characters do something which is different from what they do on the physical plane. Yet they are alive, they *do* something. But if we transfer naturalistic plays into the spiritual world, the characters are like wooden dolls. They have no life, can neither stand nor walk—they can do nothing at all, because they are not alive.'

A recent book on Shakespeare's characters, by John O'Connor, offers remarkable testimony to this even in its title: *Shakespearean Afterlives—Ten Characters with a Life of their Own.* It notes (on the cover): 'The seemingly endless capacity of [Shakespeare's] characters for re-invention and reincarnation.'

9 Owen Barfield, for example writes in 'The Form of Hamlet', in *Romanticism Comes of Age,* about the 'uneasy feeling' one may have that Shakespeare: '...does not mean anything. He has nothing to say. His characters know what they mean and can utter it in the most beautiful language. They know also what they want, have individuality. Not so the author. He is, indeed, "not one but all mankind's epitome". He has no existence apart from the characters.'

In Jorge Luis Borges' fable, *Everything and Nothing,* God famously compares Shakespeare to Himself, addressing him face to face as '...my Shakespeare... who like myself are many and no one'.

Rudolf Steiner, who, from his spiritual-scientific research, discussed the previous incarnations of many historical individuals, never did so with regard to Shakespeare. He did, however, do so in relation to one of Shakespeare's characters, Hamlet. (*The Gospel of St Mark*, lecture 1.) This seems entirely appropriate to this riddle about Shakespeare's being.

10 Southworth, op.cit., p.9.

Chapter 2

1 Rudolf Steiner: *From Symptom to Reality in Modern History*, Lectures 1 & 2.

2 Charles Williams, (in *James I*, p. 50) describing King James at 17, writes tellingly of this hidden aspect to him:

'The King now had a trick, 'far beyond his own wont', of himself keeping the key of the coffer wherein his papers lay, 'so as hitherto', Bowes [an English agent in Scotland] added, 'I cannot get any certainty of the contents'. It was a permanent alteration; he locked his coffer; he locked the more secret coffer of his mind—the more James he.'

3 See note 1.

4 Rudolf Steiner: *The Karma of Untruthfulness Vol. 1*, p. 241.

5 A little later, for example, Steiner tells us that until the time of the Renaissance 'commerce was still just under the influence of the spiritual world', but that around the time of the advent of our modern age 'everything commercial was drawn over into the occult sphere which is guided by the so-called 'Brothers of the Shadow'. For further discussion of James I's relationship to these Western 'brotherhoods' see Sergei Prokoffief: *The Spiritual Origins of Eastern Europe and the Future Mysteries of the Holy Grail*, pp.197, 324 & 326, and endnotes 111 (p.464) and 181, 183 & 186 (pp.520–521). (Prokoffief, however, does not discuss the other, very different side of James's activity.)

6 Rudolf Steiner: *Toward Imagination*.

7 Steiner describes two one-sidednesses, or 'evils', which constantly exert their sway on us. One attempts to draw us only into the realm of the spirit, away from all earthly reality, the other to bind us only to earthly, material realities. Steiner named the first tendency 'luciferic', after the spiritual being Lucifer, from Hebrew tradition, and the second 'ahrimanic', after the spiritual being Ahriman, from Persian tradition. Ahriman—or Mammon—is clearly the more prominent of the two in our own culture. The human being is challenged to find the true ground that holds these two one-sidednesses in balance.

8 See note 7.

9 Rudolf Steiner: *The Karma of Untruthfulness Vol. 2*, p. 131.

10 'Fifth post Atlantean period' is a term Steiner uses for the modern era in which we are living, beginning around the time of the Renaissance in the 15th century, and seen as extending over at least the whole of the present millennium.

11 Rudolf Steiner: *The Karma of Untruthfulness Vol. 1*, p. 236.

12 This and succeeding quotations: Rudolf Steiner: *The Karma of Untruthfulness Vol. 2*, pp. 129–131.

13 Quotation at bottom of page 19: 'One of the greatest ...'.

14 See note 9.

15 Rudolf Steiner: *Karmic Relationships, Vol. 2*, Lecture 2, pp. 28–29.

16 Rudolf Steiner: *Toward Imagination*, pp. 158–159.

17 Rudolf Steiner: *Gegenwärtiges und Vergangenes im Menschengeiste*, 28 March 1916, p. 57. GA 167. (My translation.)

18 Rudolf Steiner, *Toward Imagination*, p. 132.

19 *Toward Imagination*, pp. 157–8. These 'two main streams' Steiner is speaking of come to expression in Jesuitism and Freemasonry, represented by Francisco Suarez and James I respectively.

20 The Renaissance—commonly seen as the beginning of the 'modern era' and of the 'scientific age'—led to, and paradoxically was itself the result of a massive change in human consciousness. Shakespeare and Bacon are almost archetypally representative of this change, which involves, among other

things, a more detached awareness of the world, leading to a greater sense of human individuality and of the physical world. Rudolf Steiner describes that a new soul faculty began to emerge in humanity at this time, which he termed the '*consciousness soul*'. There is perhaps no greater portrayal of this newly emerging consciousness than we find in *Hamlet*. (For a remarkable and sensitive study of *Hamlet*, in relation to the 'consciousness soul', see Owen Barfield's essay: 'The Form of Hamlet' in *Romanticism Comes of Age*.)

21 The only place, to my knowledge, where Steiner mentioned James I after this is in some comments he made following a lecture by Count Ludwig Polzer-Hoditz, on 23 June 1920. There Steiner says: 'The real outer bearer [of this English politics] is King James I.' (GA 337a—my translation.)

22 From: *Historical Characters and their Place in Evolution—Bacon, Shakespeare, Boehme, Balde*, Rudolf Steiner, lecture of 1 February 1920. Printed in supplement to *Anthroposophical Movement* (6) Vol IX. No. 18 (GA 196). (There follow a series of quotations from the same lecture.)

23 Steiner adds: 'And it might happen in an extreme case of this kind that centuries afterwards the memoirs of such a person are discovered and found to contain ideas and impulses which, although they had never made their way into literature, were yet characteristic precisely of his time.'

24 Albert Steffen: 'Letzte Stunden bei Rudolf Steiner', in *Das Goetheanum*, 12 April 1925, p. 113. (I am grateful to Johannes Kiersch for sending me this passage.)

25 Das Neue Jahrhundert. Eine Tragödie von Otto Borngräber', *Magazin für Literatur*, 1900, 69, in: *Gesammelte Aufsätze zur Dramaturgie 1889–1900*, GA 29.

26 James I was born on 19 June 1566 and died on 27 March 1625. Coincidentally, or not, Steiner mentioned James I for the first time in a lecture on almost exactly the same day—28 March (1916).

27 In *The Karma of Untruthfulness*, Vol. 1, and in the lecture of

October 1919. Even in these places there are definite riddles regarding *what* Steiner is saying about James.

28   A name given to students of Rudolf Steiner's spiritual science, which he also termed 'anthroposophy', meaning 'the wisdom of the human being'. Thomas Vaughan—twin brother of the poet Henry Vaughan—was possibly the first to use this word, publishing his *Anthroposophia Theomagia* in 1650.

29   M. Bennell and I. Wyatt in: *Shakespeare's Flowering of the Spirit.* Isabel Wyatt in: 'James I' (essay), in *The Christian Community*, Vol. IV, nos. 9 and 10, Sept/Oct. 1950; K. Koenig: *Darwin*, (handwritten notes for a lecture given on 21 Feb, 1952. Camphill Archives); E. Lehrs: *The Rosicrucian Foundations of The Age of Natural Science* (essay), tr. Mabel Cotterell, (available from Rudolf Steiner House Library, London). Francis Edmunds nowhere, to my knowledge, expressed this anywhere in writing. His last book, however, *The Quest for Meaning*—a study of modern science—avoids any direct discussion of Francis Bacon, precisely because Edmunds had become unclear about Bacon's relationship to Christian Rosenkreutz. A. C. Harwood also never expresses this view explicitly, but implies it in a review of Frances Yates's *The Rosicrucian Enlightenment.* He speaks of the many references which 'connect Bacon with the Rosicrucian stream'. (*Anthroposophical Quarterly*, Vol. 18, No. 2, Summer 1973, p. 46.)

30   Rudolf Steiner: *The Temple Legend*, p. 53 and note 5, p. 322.

31   German original: 'In der Zeit, als Bacon, Shakespeare, Jakob Böhme und noch ein anderer gewirkt haben, ein Eingeweihter da war.'

32   The scant historical records that do exist about the Comte de St. Germain range between the years 1710 and 1822. (Isabel Cooper-Oakley: *The Count of Saint Germain*, p. 27.)

33   A great deal is, of course, known about Jakob Balde, only not in Britain. (See Jakob Balde bibliography on www.klassphil.uni-muenchen.de/~stroh/balde-bib.htm).

Particularly intriguing for our theme is the description of a poem of Balde's which spells out, acrostically: 'Before I wrote this, I was writing on the other side of the ocean. That was after Shakespeare died.' ('Bevor ich dieses schrieb, schrieb ich jenseits des Ozeans. Das war, nachdem Shakespeare gestorben war.') This is described in Ludwig Kleeberg: *Wege und Worte— Erinnerungen an Rudolf Steiner aus Tagebüchern und Briefen*, pp. 159–160. This volume also contains what, to my knowledge, is the first recorded description of Steiner discussing this fourfold common inspiration. Kleeberg tells us how in *1907* Steiner had told him that: 'Bacon and Shakespeare, as well as Jakob Böhme and Jakobus Baldus were all inspired by the same Master'. (I am grateful to Harald Hamre for pointing out this passage.)

34 Thus in the lecture 'The European Mysteries and their Initiates' Rudolf Steiner says: 'Profound achievements of spiritual life were influenced by the mysterious threads of Rosicrucianism which found their way into civilization. So, for instance, there is a connection between Bacon of Verulam's *New Atlantis* and Rosicrucianism.' (*Anthroposophical Quarterly*, Vol. 9, No. 1, Spring 1964.)

Frances Yates says, similarly: 'There are undeniably influences from the *Fama* in the *New Atlantis*.' This is far from saying, though, that all of Bacon's works are the result of the direct inspiration of Christian Rosenkreutz. We should rather see this, I believe, as the furthest Steiner was able to go in speaking about Bacon's connection with Rosicrucianism. In 1901 Marie von Sivers had sent Steiner an article from *The Theosophical Review* entitled: 'Reasons for Believing Francis Bacon a Rosicrucian.' Steiner had replied: 'The article about Bacon is very interesting [...] But I feel rather strongly that the writer treats the whole matter somewhat lightly, as I cannot share the view that Bacon's philosophical writings have an esoteric meaning. This is surely necessary if he is to be treated as a Rosicrucian.' (From: *Rudolf Steiner—Marie Steiner-von Sivers. Correspondence and Documents 1901–1925*, letter of 13 April 1901, p. 23.)

35 Similar to the general assumption in Britain that Steiner was referring to Rosenkreutz behind Bacon and Shakespeare, there is an aprocryphal tale in Continental Europe that Rudolf Steiner

once stated that Christian Rosenkreutz was the 'stranger' who visited Jacob Boehme in his youth. Even if he was, there is no evidence that Rudolf Steiner ever said this.

36 In March 1916 Steiner said: 'James worked with immense influence, over wide distances' In 1924 he said the troublesome patron was: 'An individuality from whom immense forces proceeded.'

37 Peter Dawkins: *Francis Bacon, Herald of a New Age*, p. 51.

38 Rudolf Steiner: *The Karma of Untruthfulness Vol. 1*, p. 238.

39 See Frances Yates: *The Rosicrucian Enlightenment*, Ch. 1, 'A Royal Wedding'; also Joy Hancox: *Kingdom for a Stage, Magicians and Aristocrats in Elizabethan Theatre*, p. 24.

40 E.g. Joy Hancox, ibid., Ch.10, 'Out of the Shadows'.

41 Adrian Gilbert: *The New Jerusalem*, p. 48: 'Thus the stream of thought that Baconism represented in England was not merely sympathetic to Continental Rosicrucianism, in many ways it was identical with it.' Frances Yates in *The Rosicrucian Enlightenment* (p. 180) similarly speaks of: 'A movement which [...] developed as Baconianism in England, as Rosicrucianism in Germany.'

42 Frances Yates: *Theatre of the World*, pp. 65–66: 'James is addressed as "Ter Maximus", Emperor of the heavens and the earth, a shining ray of the divine light, to whom the truths of Nature revealed in the book are dedicated, which open a way to the heavens as by Jacob's Ladder, and are presented to the representative of the Deity on earth, King James.' This leads Yates to question: 'What encouraged Fludd to believe that James I would be interested in his *Utriusque Cosmi Historia*?' (I discuss this more fully in Chapter Six.)

43 Gilbert, op. cit., p. 64.

44 Lomas op. cit., p. 80.

Chapter 3

1 *The Advancement of Learning*, ed. Stephen Jay Gould, p. 5.

2 Ibid. p. 168.

3 Ibid. p. 4.

4 This and previous quotation from: Francis Bacon: *The New Organon*, ed. Jardine and Silverthorne, p. 4.

5 Peter Dawkins sees Solamona as Bacon: 'Bacon, the second Solomon, calls his Temple the House of Solomon [...] founded by himself in the guise of Solamona (i.e. Solomon II)' (*Building Paradise*, p. 142). Adrian Gilbert argues that: 'The wise King Solamona [...] is intended to be symbolic of James I himself.' (op. cit. p. 142.) John Henry argues along the same lines as Gilbert: 'Establishing Solomon's House, we are told, was the pre-eminent act of its wisest king.' (*Knowledge is Power—How Magic, the Government and an Apocalyptic Vision Inspired Francis Bacon to Create Modern Science*, p. 123.) Dawkins tells us that: 'Bacon always hoped that King James would become, or at least, act like Solomon, but in fact James always referred to his Lord Chancellor, Bacon, as his Solomon.' (*Building Paradise* p. 60.) I can find no supporting evidence for this last remark.

6 From: *Francis Bacon, The Major Works*, pp. 469–471.

7 Joseph Devey (ed.): *The Moral and Historical Works of Lord Bacon*, Introduction, p. xxiv.

8 Letter of 8 October 1621.

9 Letter of 21 April, 1621.

10 Letter from Bacon to James, 20 October 1620, quoted in Lisa Jardine's Introduction to *The New Organon*, op. cit. p. xxvii.

11 Introduction to *The New Organon*, p. xxvii.

12 Spedding (ed.): *Life & Letters of Francis Bacon, Vol. 14*, p. 327.

13 Ibid. Letter on *Novum Organon*, 12 Oct. 1620, p. 120.

14 Ibid. Unsent letter to the King, 1621, p. 382.

15 Act 4, sc.III, 1.156.

16 *Measure for Measure*, Introduction, p. 50.

17 George Walton Williams: 'Macbeth, King James' Play', *South Atlantic Review*, 47.2, 1982.

18 Henry Paul: *The Royal Play of Macbeth*.

19 See Godfrey Watson: *Bothwell and the Witches*.

20 See *Macbeth*, Act IV, Scenes 1 and 4—'the two scenes which

would most particularly appeal to King James'. (Muriel Bradbrook, 'Origins of *Macbeth*', MacMillan Casebook on *Macbeth*, p.
243.)

21 Jane H. Jack: 'Macbeth, King James and the Bible', *Journal of
English Literary History*, pp. 173–193.)

22 Ted Hughes: *Shakespeare and the Goddess of Complete Being*, p. 243.

23 MacMillan Casebook on *Macbeth*, ed. John Wain, p. 30.

24 Leah Marcus: 'Cymbeline and the Unease of Topicality' in
Shakespeare and the Last Plays, p. 136. *The Tempest*, which was one
of the plays performed at the wedding celebrations of Princess
Elizabeth and Frederick the Elector Palatine, has also attracted
political comment of this kind. Much of this is about the Masque
within the play celebrating the betrothal of the royal pair, Mir-
anda and Ferdinand. This also extends to comparisons between
Miranda's father, Prospero, and Elizabeth's father, King James.
David Bevington writes, for example ('The Tempest and the
Jacobean Court Masque' in Bevington and Holbrook (eds.), *The
Politics of the Stuart Court Masque*): 'In so far as the play invites the
Jacobean spectator to ponder James's role as monarch through
the image of Prospero, the portrait is not uniformly flattering.
Recent critical views of Prospero as indulgent and yet irritatingly
managerial, learned and yet foolishly inattentive to public
responsibility, visionary about peace and yet impolitic as a ruler,
all find inviting parallels in current historical debates about
James.'

25 Alvin Kernan: *Shakespeare, the King's Playwright, Theatre in the
Stuart Court, 1603–1613.*

26 Kernan dares to suggest an outer connection to James even in
Hamlet, which was written before 1603. No one else I know of has
spoken of a link with James *before* his arrival in England. Should
we wish to do so we need, I think, to contemplate an inner
influence; or, which is admittedly difficult, but constantly
attempted by Ted Hughes in *Shakespeare and the Goddess of
Complete Being* (though not in relation to James), to speak of
Shakespeare's work being influenced from its own future.

27 Philip C. McGuire: *Shakespeare, The Jacobean Plays*, p. 29.

28 Lepanto was the place of a massive sea battle in 1571 in which the 'Christian alliance' had overcome the Turks.

29 Kernan, op. cit. p. 61.

30 'Othello: an Introduction', Alvin B. Kernan, in Kernan (ed.): *Modern Shakespearean Criticism*, p. 359.

31 Most of the comments on Shakespeare's work I have referred to in this chapter have severe limitations, in my opinion, as literary criticism. They have been chosen, of course, because of what they have to say about this historical connection and context within Shakespeare.

Chapter 4

1 'To the Great Variety of Readers', First Folio, 1623.

   W. B. Yeats tells us of a visionary experience someone had of Shakespeare, in the midst of his creativity. Even if only as a poetic picture, it addresses our awe and amazement on trying to imagine the sheer *intensity* of Shakespeare's creative life: 'Thomas Lake Harris, the half-charlatan American visionary, said of Shakespeare: "Often the hair of his head stood up and all life became the echoing chambers of the tomb." ' W. B. Yeats: *A Vision*, p. 153.

2 Steiner wrote what may be seen as his first spiritual-scientific work, *Christianity as Mystical Fact*, in 1902.

3 See page 23, Chapter 2.

4 Friedrich Hiebel was the first, as far as I am aware, to state that James I was the initiate to whom Steiner was referring. He discusses this extensively in his *Das Drama des Dramas*, Part 2, Chapters 3, 4 and 5. Chapter 3 is entitled: 'About Shakespeare's Source of Inspiration. King James 1.' I only discovered Hiebel's book after arriving at my own conclusions on this. I am happy that I first made my own discoveries, but was also very heartened to find that in Central Europe another had so expressly stated what I had become convinced of. Retrospectively, therefore, I offer all due acknowledgement to Hiebel's work.

5 I am aware that I do not discuss in this volume the claims that have been made for other supposed authors of Shakespeare— e.g. Edward de Vere (Earl of Oxford) or Christopher Marlowe. Much as 'Oxfordians' or 'Marlovians' may disagree with me, however, it must, I think, be recognized that the central debate relating to authorship focuses on Francis Bacon. The first public conference of the Shakespearian Authorship Trust may be seen, in the end, to have confirmed this. The main speaker defending the case of William Shakespeare admitted that he himself was not of the opinion that Shakespeare wrote the plays; the main speaker for Christopher Marlowe described many remarkable and fascinating connections between the works of Marlowe and Shakespeare, but admitted he was not seriously suggesting that Marlowe *wrote* Shakespeare; the main speaker for the Earl of Oxford regaled the audience with wonderful tales about the Earl of Oxford, remarking that even if Oxford *hadn't* written Shakespeare, we would surely admit that it makes an excellent story that he did. The case for Mary Sidney having written the plays provided, perhaps, the most ejoyable presentation, without too many—presumably—literally believing it to be true. As a result it was only Francis Bacon who was wholly seriously and committedly believed by his advocate (Peter Dawkins) to be the true author of the works of Shakespeare.

We find something similar, as described in the Introduction, towards the end of John Michell's book *Who Wrote Shakespeare?*.

6 Peter Dawkins: *Francis Bacon, Herald of the New Age*, p. 47.

7 Rudolf Steiner: *Karmic Relationships, Vol 2*, p. 29.

8 Lecture of 9 October 1912, in: www.sirbacon.org

9 From the front cover of Peter Dawkins: *Building Paradise, The Freemasonic and Rosicrucian Six Days Work*.

10 Gilbert, op. cit., p. 145.

11 See Rudolf Steiner (ed. Christopher Bamford): *The Secret Stream, Christian Rosenkreutz and Rosicrucianism*.

12 One of the signatures of Christian Rosenkreutz, says Steiner, is his very rare appearance on the *outer* stage of history—the events

of his life therefore being unknown to all but the tiniest handful of individuals. Only some hundred years after his death do these events sometimes become more widely known; for example, details of the life of Christian Rosenkreutz which ended in 1484 began to emerge around 1604.

13 Dawkins: *Francis Bacon, Herald of the New Age*, p. 51.

14 Gilbert, op. cit., p. 148.

15 Gilbert may well have got his idea from Dawkins. Gilbert, who directly acknowledges Dawkins's ideas, says elsewhere: 'Many people believe him [Bacon] to have been the inspiration all along for the creation of the myth of Christian Rosenkreutz.' Op. cit., p. 148.

16 Dawkins, op. cit., p. 56.

17 When this sentence was written I was not aware of Dawkins's belief that Francis Bacon was the reincarnation of the 14th century Christian Rosenkreutz. (See final endnote of this chapter.) The sentence is still completely valid, however, for Dawkins shows no awareness of the true activity of Christian Rosenkreutz at the time of Francis Bacon, which is—at the risk of repeating myself—quite different from that of Francis Bacon.

18 For an excellent and profound study of the relationship between Shakespeare's late plays and Rosicrucianism, and particularly of *The Tempest* to *The Chymical Wedding of Christian Rosenkreutz*, see: John O'Meara: *Prospero's Powers*.

19 Steiner tells us for example that Christian Rosenkreutz himself, in the 15th Century, was responsible for imparting the Temple Legend, concerning Hiram Abiff and the building of Solomon's Temple, which later took such a central place within Freemasonry: 'What was taught by Christian Rosenkreutz could not be imparted to many people, but it was embodied in a kind of myth. Since it was first given out in the fifteenth century, it has often been repeated and explained in the various brotherhoods.' From: 'The Mystery Known to Rosicrucians' (lecture of 4 November 1904) in Rudolf Steiner, *The Temple Legend*.

20 In the chapter 'The Birth and Adoption of Francis Bacon'

Dawkins writes: 'But what of Francis's birth, the first-born son of Queen Elizabeth and Lord Robert Dudley? His birth, like the Queen's marriage, was carefully and forcefully covered up, and the Queen never did openly acknowledge Francis, or her second son Robert, as her children.' (Peter Dawkins: *Dedication to the Light*, F.B.R.T. Journal, Series 1, Volume 3). Joy Hancox also holds the view that Francis Bacon was the illegitimate child of Queen Elizabeth and Robert Dudley. See: *Kingdom for a Stage*, pp. 195–209.

Elsewhere Dawkins writes (*Building Paradise*, note 10, Ch. 7, p. 200.): 'If Francis Bacon were truly the eldest and only living son of Queen Elizabeth, as the evidence seems to indicate, then Francis would have been the legal heir to the throne of England, not James Stewart. James, therefore, could rightly be called a usurper.'

Bacon in fact set very great store by the fact that in James's person were united the thrones of England and Scotland. He wrote in a letter: 'His Majesty now of England is of more power than any of his predecessors ... his Majesty hath brought another whole kingdom to England.' (Spedding, ed.: *Life & Letters of Francis Bacon*, pp. 22–23, Vol VII.)

Soon after James arrived in England Bacon wrote an extensive 'Brief Discourse Touching the Happy Union of the Kingdoms of England and Scotland. Dedicated in private to his Majesty.' He says there: 'Your Majesty is the first king that had the honour to be *lapis angularis* [the cornerstone], to unite these two mighty and warlike nations of England and Scotland under one sovereignty and monarchy.'

Had Bacon indeed been King of England, as Dawkins would have wished, what Bacon saw as this 'Happy Union' would obviously not have taken place. Bacon was clearly not also the rightful King of Scotland. It is good to know that even Dawkins's extravagant claims have limits. Even he has not yet so far suggested that Bacon could have been the son both of Elizabeth I *and* of Mary, Queen of Scots.

21 Arthur Conan Doyle, by contrast, who was a born story-teller, declared in Shakespeare's own voice, after seeing Bacon's verse for the first time, that it provides us with the best evidence that Bacon could not have written Shakespeare. The piece is called: *Shakespeare's Exposition*, and Conan Doyle has Shakespeare, uneasy in his grave on account of Bacon's claims, answer the charges:

You prate about my learning. I would urge
My want of learning rather as proof
That I am still myself. Have I not traced
A seaboard to Bohemia, and made
The cannons war a whole wide century
Before the first was forged? Think you, then,
That he, the ever-learned Verulam,
Would have erred thus?
[...]
They say that they have found
A script, wherein the writer tells my Lord
He is a secret poet. True enough!
But surely now that secret is o'er past.
Have you not read his poems? Know you not
That in our day a learned chancellor
Might far better dispense unjustest law
Than be suspect of such frivolity
As lies in verse? Therefore his poetry
Was secret. Now that he is gone
'Tis so no longer. You may read his verse,
And judge if mine be better or be worse: Read and pronounce!

I find it difficult to believe that Bacon himself would ever have argued with this relative judgement of his poetry. He wrote to Fulke Greville, offering him advice for his studies: 'Of the choice ... I think history of most, and I had almost said of only use. For poets, I can commend none, being resolved to be ever a stran-

ger to them.' (*Francis Bacon, The Major Works*, p. 105.) No doubt
Baconians would say he was deliberately concealing himself, but
they must, I believe, honestly ask themselves whether this is in
fact the case.

22 See note 34, Chapter Two.

23 See Dawkins, *Francis Bacon, Herald of a New Age*, p. 52, and note to
illustration 50, page x.

24 'Together with other great works veiled under adopted names,
such as Spenser, Marlowe. etc.' (Dawkins, ibid., p. 98.)

25 All these claims are found expressed, in identical terms, on a
website bearing the heading *Freemasonry in the USA*. Its aims, it
says, are to: 'Establish with ongoing research groups throughout
the world's Masonic jurisdictions that the Most Worshipful
Francis Bacon (Tudor—16th Century A.D.)

1. Is known to be the secret founder and Grand Father of
modern speculative freemasonry.

2. Is known to be the secret ruler and then Imperator (Ruler—
King) of the Worldwide Rosicrucian Order, the Ancient and
Mystical Order Rosae Crucis.

3. Is known to be the secret author of the literary works of
William Shakespeare, Edmund Spenser, Cervantes (*Don
Quixote*), the King James translation of the Holy Bible, and
the Charters of the Virginia Colonies (then to be the United
States of America...)

It gives his name throughout as 'Francis Bacon (Tudor)',
asserting, like Dawkins, that he was the 'lawful son of Queen
Elizabeth I of England, and heir to the throne'.
(www.capidea.com/the_sacred_trust.htm)

26 Dawkins, *Francis Bacon, Herald of a New Age*, p. 59. Dawkins
describes this as a view held 'in some quarters', but is himself
clearly to be seen as one of those quarters.

27 Dawkins, ibid., p. xiii.

28 See the many examples we have given in Chapter Three of
Bacon's lauding of King James. Charles Williams compared the
attitudes of those who endlessly see the bad in James with that of

Francis Bacon, who 'daily accustomed to him [...] beheld continually emerging from that fantastic circle the lofty and immaculate figure of the elect of God, the sovereign and serene prince of justice and wisdom'. (Charles Williams: *James I*, p. 254.)

29 Gilbert, op. cit., p. 128.

30 See note 33, Chapter Two.

31 *The Rosicrucian Enlightenment*, p. 239 & p. 32.

32 Ibid. p. 221.

33 In *Kingdom for a Stage*, Chapter 9, Hancox sets out to show that the *real* purpose of the German Rosicrucian author Theophilus Schweighardt's *Account of the Rosic. Fraternity* was to point to the spiritual primacy of Francis Bacon.

An exception to this tendency among British writers on Rosicrucianism is Christopher McIntosh. He devotes a chapter in his book *The Rosicrucians*, for example, to 'The Esoteric Tradition in Germany'. He also attempts to rectify some of the exaggerated claims that have been made about John Dee and Francis Bacon: 'Her [Frances Yates's] claims about Dee's role [in Rosicrucianism] appear exaggerated in the light of recent scholarship' (p.29); 'Bacon's connection with the Rosicrucians has been exaggerated to extraordinary proportions by certain people' (p.40).

34 We might smilingly note that the fact that Jakob Boehme 'transforms the whole inspiration into the soul substance of Central Europe' is a story told to us in his name, which means James of Bohemia, or: Bohemian James.

For more on James's outwardly visible links with Bohemia see Chapter Six—'Rudolf II.'

35 Wallace-Murphy & Hopkins: *Rosslyn*, p. 196. (The village of *Roslin*, near Edinburgh, is the site of Rosslyn Chapel.)

36 Cf. Dawkins: *Building Paradise*, p. 59. Bacon, according to Dawkins, 'was a master of Cabala, and the whole project of his Great Instauration is designed accordingly'. (Ibid, p. 59.)

For a brief description of the history of Cabala—'Kabbalah' in Hebrew—and of its influence in British cultural life, at least since the 16th Century, see Adrian Gilbert: *The New Jerusalem*, pp. 200–206. Gilbert describes Cabala as one method of studying the 'Perennial Philosophy', and as having 'much in common with [...] the Egyptian *Hermetica*'. The 'perennial philosophy' and the *Hermetica*, or ancient Hermeticism, both upheld so strongly within Britain, have this same character of: 'ancient knowledge passed down the generations'.

37 Lecture of 28 March 1916—from: *Gegenwärtiges und Vergangenes im Menschengeiste*, GA 167. (My translation.)

38 'The Nature and Significance of Goethe's Writings on Organic Development', in Rudolf Steiner: *Goethean Science*, Mercury Press, New York 1988, p. 76.

39 Lecture of 26 October 1917 in *The Fall of the Spirits of Darkness*, Rudolf Steiner Press, London, 1993.

40 *The Temple Legend*, p. 241.

41 By connecting with 'the whole of the rest of European culture' James I takes on what Walter Johannes Stein describes as the true role of King Arthur: '... there have been many King Arthurs and the title was given to all those who honoured and worked for the continuity of the island kingdom in such a way that the progress and evolution of other nations were included.' *The Death of Merlin*, W.J. Stein, pp. 115–116.

It is essential that we understand, however, that what was given to the world at the beginning of the 17th Century, through the immense co-working of William Shakespeare, Francis Bacon and Jakob Boehme, in particular, is not simply valid for all time, but has evolved, and must continue to do so. Thus Rudolf Steiner remarks: 'To a large extent the direction and attitude of modern thinking go back to the beginning of the fifth post-Atlantean epoch, when the predominating spirit lived in the accomplishments of Bacon, Shakespeare and Jakob Boehme. This had to be so. However, we are now at a point where we have to overcome what was rightfully inaugurated [then].' *Toward Imagination*, Rudolf Steiner, p. 132.

42 T.S. Eliot in the 20th Century is a perhaps unlikely example of

this kind of collaboration. As editor of Faber & Faber he published Ernst Lehrs's book *Man or Matter* (Faber, 1951), an in-depth study and overview of the implications for science of Goethe's scientific work. Eliot also published the books of Owen Barfield who, profoundly influenced by Goethe and Rudolf Steiner, examined the scientific and philosophical under-pinnings of present-day culture. See *History in English Words* (Faber, 1926), *Poetic Diction* (Faber, 1928), *Saving the Appearances* (Faber, 1957), *Worlds Apart* (Faber, 1963). Eliot also published the books of Charles Waterman, who, inspired by Steiner's social and political insights after the First World War, offered a radical rethinking of British society after the Second World War: *The Three Spheres of Society* (Faber, 1946). In response to C.P. Snow's discussion of the 'Two Cultures' of art and science, and the growing divide between them, Waterman also wrote *Towards a Third Culture* (Faber, 1961). Eliot himself, interviewed on German radio, commented: 'It seems to me that Goethe had a compass of consciousness which far surpassed that of his 19th Century contemporaries. Rudolf Steiner expressly upheld this, and I do too.' (Nordwest-Deutscher Rundfunk, 1957.)

43 *Consensus Design*, Christopher Day, Architectural Press, Oxford, 2003.

44 'Without what I have learned from her [Margaret Colquhoun], there would be no process method and no book....,' says Day, adding in a footnote: 'Her method in turn was based on Dr Jochen Bockemuehl's [...], the inspiration for which stretches back to Rudolf Steiner and Goethe, before him.' *Consensus Design*, Christopher Day (Acknowledgements and p. 6.).

45 Taken from: Rudolf Steiner: *Die geistigen Hintergründe des ersten Weltkrieges.* (tr. 'The Spiritual Origins of the First World War'), GA 174b, Rudolf Steiner Verlag, Dornach, 1994, lecture of 12 March 1916.

46 After this chapter had been written I discovered the statements of a number of leading British theosophists regarding the supposed previous incarnations of Francis Bacon, which attempt to

show, by a different route, that Bacon and Christian Rosenkreutz are the same individual. Thus Annie Besant in 1912 said that the 'Master R' or the 'Master Rákóczy' was: '... known as the Comte de Saint-Germain in the history of the 18th century, as Bacon in the 17th, as Robertus the monk in the 16th, as Hunyadi János in the 15th, as Christian Rosenkreutz in the 14th—to take a few of his incarnations...'

C. W. Leadbeater repeated this in a book of 1925 (*The Masters and the Path*): 'The Master the Comte de St. Germain, known to history in the eighteenth century, whom we sometimes call the Master Rákóczi [...] was Francis Bacon, Lord Verulam, in the seventeenth century, Robertus the monk in the sixteenth, Hunyadi Janos in the fifteenth, Christian Rosenkreutz in the fourteenth, and Roger Bacon in the thirteenth [...] Further back in time he was the great Neoplatonist Proclus, and before that St. Alban.'

Alice Bailey in her 1922 book, *Initiation, Human and Solar*, also states this: 'The Master who concerns himself especially with the future development of racial affairs in Europe, and with the mental outgrowth in America and Australia is the Master Rákóczy [...] he was particularly before the public eye when he was the Comte de Saint-Germain, and earlier still when he was both Roger Bacon and later, Francis Bacon. It is interesting to note that as the Master R takes hold, on the inner planes, of affairs in Europe, his name as Francis Bacon is coming before the public eye in the Bacon-Shakespeare controversy.' (All quoted by Dawkins in: *The Master*, Part One.)

This conflicts with the research of Rudolf Steiner, who described the very hidden activities of Christian Rosenkreutz during Francis Bacon's lifetime. (See lecture of 18 December 1912, for example, in *The Secret Stream*.) He would almost certainly not have been known by name as Christian Rosenkreutz, but was very definitely, according to Steiner, a completely separate individual from Francis Bacon.

Rudolf Steiner, Annie Besant, C. W. Leadbeater and Alice

Bailey all state that the Comte de St Germain was a reincarnation of Christian Rosenkreutz. Apart from that one instance, however, Steiner's statements and those of the latter three differ radically. Steiner's research revealed quite different spiritual backgrounds of Christian Rosenkreutz on the one hand and Francis Bacon on the other.

Without going into any of the details of this, which readers may pursue for themselves, one may at least say that central to Rudolf Steiner's picture, which Besant, Leadbeater and Bailey say nothing about, is Christian Rosenkreutz's intimate connection, as his name suggests, with the incarnation of Christ. This is hinted at in the *Fama,* which calls Christian Rosenkreutz: 'granum pectori Jesu insitum' – a seed planted in Jesus's breast.

The picture given by Besant, Leadbeater and Bailey is not, I believe, a true series of incarnations at all, despite the genuine link between Christian Rosenkreutz and the Comte de St Germain. There are simply too many nominal connections to Bacon—St Alban, Roger Bacon, Francis Bacon—and too many Englishmen—four altogether, these three and Robertus the monk, presumably either 'Robertus Anglicus' or Robert of Chester. Neither of them, it should be noted, actually lived in the 16th century. The most likely candidate for Robertus would appear to be Robert of Chester (Castrensis) whose work appeared in the 16th century, but who lived in the 12th century. Robertus is famous for translating the works of Morienus from Arabic into Latin. Morienus is known for teaching alchemy to the Caliph Mu'awijah, thereby bringing alchemy to Arabia.

The furthest back this line goes is, tellingly, to St Alban, claimed by Freemasons as the founder of Freemasonry ('The first Grand Master, AD 287, Saint Alban', according to the *Royal Masonic Cyclopaedia,* quoted in Dawkins, op.cit. p.89.) The second connection is with the Neoplatonist Proclus (AD 412–485). What we are given, I believe, is a statement of spiritual and cultural affiliation, rather than a genuinely perceived series of incarnations. This statement, furthermore, has a clear political-spiritual intention, and one which would draw not only Christian Rosenkreutz but also the Comte de St Germain into the Baconian (from St Albans through Roger Bacon to Francis Bacon), Freemasonic and British domain. In Alice Bailey's final sentence one can even catch a glimpse of the part played in all this by the seemingly harmless 'Bacon–Shakespeare controversy' in the 'public eye'.

Chapter 5

1 Williams: *Great Britain's Solomon*, quoted in: Alan Stewart: *The Cradle King, A Life of James VI and I*.

2 Much of Williams's sermon is quoted in: Caroline Bingham, *James I of England*. The following are some brief extracts: 'King Solomon is said to be *unigenitus coram matre sua*, the only son of his mother. So was King James. Solomon was an infant King, *puer parvulus*, a little child. So was King James, a King at the age of thirteen months. Solomon was twice crowned and anointed a King. So was King James. Solomon was learned above all princes of the East. So was King James above all princes of the universal world. Solomon was a writer in prose and verse. So in a very pure and exquisite manner was our sweet sovereign King James [...] Lastly, before any hostile act we read of in history, King Solomon died in peace, when he had lived about sixty years [...] and so you know did King James...'

3 *The Cradle King*, p. 52. A similar thing happened when James arrived in England in 1603. Instead of Solomon, though, a scene was played out before him where three witches declared him to be the descendant of Banquo. The event is one of the sources of *Macbeth*.

4 Such jibes excluded, James unquestionably enjoyed and even fostered the comparison, as shown by the frontispiece to his works. He has therefore been termed a 'self-styled King Solo-

mon', though it was certainly not all his own doing. In his *Meditation Upon the Lord's Prayer* James writes: 'I know not by what fortune, the *dicton* of PACIFICUS was added to my title [...] but I am not ashamed of this addition: for King *Solomon* was a figure of CHRIST in that, that he was a King of peace.' (Quoted in Roy Strong: *Britannia Triumphans*, p. 55.)

5 See footnote 5, Chapter Three.

6 1 Kings, 6, 16–18, KJB.

7 1 Kings 6, 20, KJB.

8 Crowns have their compass; length of days, their date;
   Triumphs, their tombs; felicity, her fate.
   Of more than earth can earth make none partaker,
   But knowledge makes the king most like his maker.

   The lines certainly bear comparison with many of Shakespeare's sonnets. Stanley Wells and Gary Taylor, having described how the lines appear, for the first time, unattributed, on the frontispiece, write: 'They are attributed to Shakespeare [...] in at least two seventeenth-century manuscripts; the same attribution was recorded in a printed broadside now apparently lost.' *William Shakespeare, The Complete Works*, ed. Wells and Taylor, p. 778.

9 Charles Williams: *James I*, Arthur Barker, p. 24.

10 William McElwee: *The Wisest Fool in Christendom*, p. 39.

11 Frances Yates: *The Theatre of the World*, p. 67.

12 This and previous quotation: Frances A. Yates: *Giordano Bruno and the Hermetic Tradition*, p. 399.

13 Quoted in: Alan F. Westcott (ed.), *New Poems of James I of England*, introduction, p. lxiv.

14 *The Advancement of Learning*, First Book, second paragraph.

15 Among James's writings are: *Basilikon Doron* (3 volumes), *Daemonology* (3 volumes), *The Trew Law of Free Monarchies, An Apology for the Oath of Allegiance—(Premonition to all Christian Monarchs), A Counter Blaste to Tobacco, A paraphrase of the book of Revelations* (70 pages), A Meditation on a passage from Revelations, A Meditation on a passage from Chronicles, A Meditation on a passage

from St. Matthew, A Meditation on the Lord's Prayer, A Masque (written and contrived by James in 1588 for the marriage of his ward, the daughter of Lennox to the Earl of Huntly), 2 volumes of *Collected poetry and translations* (e.g. of Psalms).

16 Rudolf Steiner: *The Temple Legend and the Golden Legend, Freemasonry & Related Occult Movements*, Lecture 5, p. 49.

17 Roy Strong, *Britannia Triumphans*, pp. 55–64.

18 Whether or not the plans for Whitehall Palace *actually* bore any resemblance to the original Solomonic buildings in Jerusalem is not the point. Strong shows exact echoes of Whitehall in buildings which were *believed* to replicate Solomon's Temple. A palace is by no means at odds, though, with Solomon's Temple. Emil Bock writes of how: 'The core of the Solomonic accomplishment [...] was the magnificent building which arose in Jerusalem.' But he makes it clear that what was *visibly* magnificent was: '... chiefly the palace constructions that surrounded the Temple, which in itself was inconspicuous'. (From: Emil Bock, *Kings and Prophets*, pp. 134–136.)

19 Lomas in fact describes William Schaw as 'the founding father of Freemasonry', but Schaw was working, as Lomas points out, in the service of King James. (Lomas: *The Invisible College*, p. 91.)

20 FBRT website: page on miniature portrait of Bacon by Nicholas Hilliard.

21 Bock, op. cit., p. 158.

22 1 Kings 7, 21–22.

23 Website: www.fbrt.org.uk (aims).

24 1 Kings 9, 3. NEB.

25 1 Kings 9, 6–8.

26 1 Kings 11, 11–13.

27 Although those who make great spiritual claims for Bacon will deny or decry what I am saying, in another sense they do not do so. If one thinks *only* of Francis Bacon, without any reference, that is, to William Shakespeare or to Christian Rosenkreutz, one cannot deny either the influence of his writings on scientific

materialism, or his significant role in both politics and Free-masonry. Regarding the latter his supporters have, of course, been the first to reveal the full extent of it. They do not, how-ever, see anything sinister in it.

By laying claim, in the way they do, to Shakespeare and Rosicrucianism, and basing so much of what they say upon them, they make tacit acknowledgement, in my opinion, of the insufficiency, even the infertility, of what is to be found in Bacon's works by themselves.

28 The case of Mme Blavatsky offers a clear analogy to this duality of James. According to Rudolf Steiner the earlier part of her work (e.g. *Isis Unveiled*) is to be seen as in close accord with Christian Rosenkreutz, even as being inspired by him, whereas other parts are often to be seen as directly at odds with true Rosicucianism. (See Rudolf Steiner, *Correspondence and Documents*, pp. 17–19.)

29 See: Sease and Schmidt-Brabant, *Paths of the Christian Mysteries*, p. 158.

30 Rudolf Steiner: *The Temple Legend*, p. 269.

31 12 October 1919, 3rd lecture of 3, GA 191. English typescript, available from Rudolf Steiner House Library, London.

Chapter 6

1 My translation.

2 Frances Yates: *The Rosicrucian Enlightenment*, p. 223.

3 J. W. Evans: *Rudolf II and his World, A Study in Intellectual History, 1576–1612*, p. 81—from which all the remaining quotations in this section are taken.

4 Frances Yates: *Theatre of the World*, 1987, pp. 65–66.

5 Ibid., p. 67.

6 Joscelyn Godwin: *Robert Fludd, Hermetic Philosopher and Surveyor of Two Worlds*, p. 9.

7 Robert C. Bald: *John Donne, A Life*, 1970.

8 Charles Williams: *James I*, Arthur Barker Ltd, 1934.

9 See for example: Kristin Rygg, *Masqued Mysteries Unmasked*.

There are also many fascinating insights on the masques in Frances Yates's work, for example in *The Theatre of the World.*

10 'Very large sums of money were spent on the masques. James I spent four thousand pounds (an enormous sum in those days) on one production in 1618.' (*Theatre of the World*, Yates, p. 85.)

11 R.J.W. Evans: *Rudolf II and his World*, p. 189.

12 From Ben Jonson: *The Complete Masques, Oberon*, 1.220.

13 For Fludd's friendships with Paddy and Harvey see Yates's *Theatre of the World* p. 64. (Same reference for brief quotation on Fludd that ends this sentence.)

14 Evans, p. 205.

15 Spedding (ed.): *Letters and Life of Francis Bacon*, Vol. 14, p. 312. Succeeding comment by Bacon on 'Paracelsus and the Alchemists' in: *Francis Bacon, The Major Works*, p. 208.

16 Frances A. Yates, *The Art of Memory*, 1978, p. 310.

17 Frances A. Yates, *Giordano Bruno and the Hermetic Tradition*, Chapter 21—'After Hermes Trismegistos was dated'—p. 398.

18 Op. cit. p. 399.

19 Robert Bald: *John Donne—A Life*, p. 283.

20 Yates comments that: 'A more total contrast than that exhibited by these two works, published within a few years of one another and both dedicated to the King of England, could hardly be imagined.' (Ibid p. 403.) What Yates cannot imagine is that this contrast could also be sustained within King James himself, and therefore decides, against all the evidence, that James was anti-Fludd.

21 Yates, *The Art of Memory*, p. 312.

22 *Advancement of Learning*, Book One, Paragraph Two, published in 1605 & 1623.

23 Yates, ibid, p. 69.

24 Joy Hancox: *The Byrom Collection*, p. 254.

25 On the *Naometria*, see Yates, *The Rosicrucian Enlightenment*, pp. 33–35; on the 'new stars' of 1604, discussed by Kepler, ibid. p. 48.

26 A characteristic noticed by Antonia Fraser: 'James showed a

felicitous taste in encouraging others to write projects.' Antonia Fraser: *King James* p. 49.

27 Yates: *The Theatre of the World*, p. 177.

28 Op. cit. p. 185.

29 In *The Art of Memory* (1966) Yates is excitedly positive about James. In *Theatre of the World* (1969) she begins to be more questioning. By the time of *The Rosicrucian Enlightenment* (1972) she has an almost wholly negative picture of James. This change of attitude echoes exactly the one she says was made by sympathisers of the Protestant movement which so disastrously made Frederick Elector Palatine the King of Bohemia. It is the thesis of the present book that this by now habitual view of James is in urgent need of reconsideration.

30 This and previous quotation, *The Art of Memory*, p. 352.

31 'The manuscript continuator at Stowe, describing the end of the [Globe] theatre, says that the rebuilding was "at the very great charge of King James…".' Quoted in E. K. Chambers, *Elizabethan Stage*, Vol. 2, p. 423.

32 Ibid. pp. 333–334.

33 *The New Jerusalem*, p. 134.

34 See: www.electricsotland.com/history/ferniehirst/3.htm for information about Robert Carr. About Carr, George Erskine and their libraries see: *English Rosicrucian Manifestos* by Adam McClean at:
http:/sociologyesoscience.com/rosicrucianmanifestos.htm/

35 This, and most of the succeeding information about Erskine's collection from: I. McCallum, *History of Sir George Erskine … and the Royal College of Physicians of Edinburgh* (www.rcpe.ac.uk/publications/articles/journal_32_3/paper_12.pdf).

36 From: 'Database of alchemical manuscripts—Scottish Libraries' on Adam McClean's website.

37 The 'Society at Hess' has been connected with the court of Moritz of Hessen-Kassel (1572–1632), often seen as a focus for alchemical and Rosicrucian interests. No evidence has been found, however, of any such figure at Moritz's court. References

have been found to a 'Dr Pellitius (Polytius)' in Wolfenbüttel, suggesting a connection to Duke Julius of Braunschweig-Wolfenbüttel (1564–1613), who is certainly someone one could imagine having a link with James. A leading patron of the time, he knew Tycho Brahe, and was close to Rudolf II in the latter's final years. He has even been compared to James, and to Rudolf II: 'Like Rudolf, Bodin and King James I he [Brunswick] combined broad intellectual horizons with a deep belief in the reality of spirits, and he was one of the foremost persecutors of witches in his day.' (*Rudolf II and his World*, Evans, p. 231.) Before moving to Prague (in 1607) he had invited English actors and writers to Wolfenbüttel, and had met Giordano Bruno there, who had dedicated two books to him.

38 Ker's copy of Schweighardt bears the same watermark as Erskine's copies of the *Fama* and the *Confessio*—the two Rosicrucian manifestos. (See: *English Rosicrucian Manifestos* by Adam McClean. Reference in note 34.)

   The third significant alchemical/Rosicrucian library of the time was that of David Lindsay, Earl of Balcarres (1585–1641). His home, Edzell Castle in Angus, had a 'Garden of the Planets', about which Adam McLean writes: 'A carved plaque over the entrance bears the date 1604 (most likely the year of its foundation), and when one remembers that James VI, who had a great interest in and was a patron of aspects of occultism, became King of the United Kingdom of Scotland and England in 1603, one realises that the building of this Mystery Temple was not taking place in a vacuum, but was part of a general renaissance of interest in hermeticism in the society of that period. Edzell was possibly a place of instruction in hermetic and alchemical philosophy and may have been a centre of Rosicrucian activity.' (Adam McLean, 'A Rosicrucian Alchemical Mystery Center in Scotland', in *The Hermetic Journal*, No.4, Summer, 1979, pp. 10–13. Quoted in McIntosh, op.cit, pp. 45-46.) McIntosh comments: 'It would appear from this that Scotland played an important and possibly key role in the early development of Rosicrucianism. This is an area of study that would clearly reward further research.'(!)

39 Anthony Holden: *William Shakespeare*, p. 206.

40 William Shakespeare: *The Complete Works*, xliv.

41 At the first public 'Shakespearean Authorship Trust' conference, held at the Globe Theatre in 2003, speakers were asked specifically to relate their arguments to this event, as a performance of *Richard II* formed part of the conference.

42 Kernan, p. 10.

43 Kernan, pp. 10 & 11.

44 Kernan, p. 11.

45 Kernan, p. 118.

46 Kernan, p. 118.

47 Carleton to Chamberlain, 7 Jan 1605—quoted in Kernan, p. 68.

48 In some versions of the story, William Herbert is told to bring the King to Wilton. Telling him 'We have the man Shakespeare with us' would obviously be the news the King was wanting to hear. In other versions the King is already at Wilton when Mary Sidney writes to her son. Either way, King James, Shakespeare and William Herbert end up together.

49 Anthony Holden: *William Shakespeare*, p. 209.

50 Kernan, xxii–xxiii. In his sensitive and sympathetic introduction to King James's poetry, Allan Westcott seems far more aware than Kernan of the deeper aspects to James's patronage, even seeming close to our own position: 'Shakespeare's position as chief dramatist of the King's company of actors, Bacon's political promotion, Donne's preferment in the church by the King's influence, and Jonson's services as composer of masques illustrate, not so much the rewards extended for literary accomplishment, as the relations with the court of the chief literary figures of the period. The general question of court patronage of the drama in the reign of James is much too complicated for brief or subordinated treatment...'. *New Poems of James I of England*, p. lvii.

51 Steve Sohmer: *The Lunar Calendar of Shakespeare's King Lear*, at: http://purl.oclc.org/emls/05-2/sohmlear.htm

52 Kernan, p. 183.

53 Charles Williams: *James I*, p. 54.

54 Wiliams, op. cit. p. 89.

55 Williams op. cit. p. 68.

56 Godfrey Watson: *Bothwell and the Witches*, pp. 121–122. James obviously survived the encounter, as did Bothwell.

57 Williams, op. cit. pp. 183–184.

58 Introduction to *Bacon's Essays and Historical Works*, Devey, p. xxvi.

59 Quoted in Southwell, op. cit. p. 275.

60 From Francis Bacon (ed. Brian Vickers): *The Major Works*, p. 787. All my information on Drebbel comes from Vickers, who expresses indebtedness to: Rosalie L Colie: *Cornelis Drebbel and Salomon de Caus: Two Jacobean Models for Salomon's House* (Huntington Library Quarterly, 18, 1954.).

61 Quoted in Kernan, op. cit. p. 73.

62 Quoted in Williams, op. cit. pp. 203–204.

63 Quoted in Williams, p. 297.

Chapter 7

1 Excluding the final 'Selah', a word with a similar function to 'Amen'.

2 Prince Henry died on 6 November 1612, and Princess Elizabeth and Frederick were married on 14 February 1613. The years when James was 23 and 46—1589/90 and 1612/1613—were both therefore of enormous importance in his biography.

I am grateful to Terry Boardman for pointing much of this out, who could, and probably should write a book on the subject. He makes a broader comment on the number 23 in *Mapping the Millennium*, pp. 174–175.

3 Letter of Oct. 1608, *Letters of King James*, ed. Akrigg. James's secret correspondence with Cecil and others, from Scotland, before his accession to the English throne, also reveals his fascination with numbers. He signed himself '30', addressed Cecil

as '10', and used other numbers to address or refer to other people.

4 New English Bible translation.

BIBLIOGRAPHY

Includes all full-length books in English referred to in the main text, and all pieces on Shakespeare. References to other shorter pieces, non-English books and web sites are included in the endnotes.

Primary Sources

Shakespeare
Craig, W.J. (ed.) *The Complete Works of William Shakespeare,* (Oxford, 1914).
Wells S. & Taylor G. (eds.) *William Shakespeare, The Complete Works* (Oxford, 1998).

Bacon
Devey, J. (ed.) *The Moral and Historical Works of Lord Bacon* (Henry Bohn, 1852).
Jardine, L. & Silverthorne, M. (eds.) *The New Organon* (OUP, 2000).
Gould, S.J. (ed.) *The Advancement of Learning* (Modern Library, 2001).
Spedding J.(ed.) *Works, Life and Letters of Francis Bacon,* Vols VII and XIV (London, 1857–1874).
Vickers, B. (ed.) *Francis Bacon, The Major Works* (Oxford World's Classics, 2002).

James I
King James I, *Workes* (London, 1616).
King James Bible (London, 1611).
Akrigg, G. (ed.) *Letters of King James* (University of California, 1984).
Westcott, A. (ed.) *New Poems of James I of England* (New York, 1966).

Secondary Sources

Shakespeare

Bennell, M. and Wyatt I., *Shakespeare's Flowering of the Spirit* (Lanthorn Press, 1971).

Bradbrook, M., 'Origins of *Macbeth*', *MacMillan Casebook on Macbeth,* ed. John Wain (Macmillan, 1969).

Granville-Barker, H., *Prefaces to Shakespeare Vol. VI* (Batsford 1974).

Hiebel, F., *Das Drama des Dramas* (Dornach, 1984).

Holden, A., *William Shakespeare* (Little, Brown & Co., 1999).

Hughes, T., *Shakespeare and the Goddess of Complete Being* (Faber, 1993).

Jack, J.H., 'Macbeth, King James and the Bible', *Journal of English Literary History* (1975).

Kernan, A., *Shakespeare, The King's Playwright, Theatre in the Stuart Court 1603–1613* (Yale, 1995).

Kernan, A., 'Othello: an Introduction', *Modern Shakespearean Criticism* (New York, 1970).

Lever, J.W., Introduction to *Measure for Measure,* (Arden, 2001).

Marcus, L., 'Cymbeline and the Unease of Topicality', *Shakespeare and the Last Plays,* ed. Ryan K. (Longman, 1999).

McGuire, P., *Shakespeare, The Jacobean Plays* (MacMillan, 1994).

Michell, J., *Who Wrote Shakespeare?* (Thames and Hudson, 2000).

O'Connor, J., *Shakespearean Afterlives, Ten Characters with a Life of Their Own* (Icon, 2003).

O'Meara, J., *Prospero's Powers* (Heart's Core, Ottawa, 2000).

Paul, H., *The Royal Play of Macbeth* (MacMillan, 1950).

Ryan, K., *Shakespeare and the Last Plays* (Longman, 1999).

Sohmer, S., 'The Lunar Calendar of Shakespeare's King Lear', *Early Modern Literary Studies* 5.2 (September 1999).

Southworth, J., *Shakespeare, The Player* (Sutton, 2000).

Wain, J. (ed.) *MacMillan Casebook on Macbeth* (Macmillan, 1969).

Walton Williams, G., 'Macbeth, King James's Play', *South Atlantic Review,* 47.2, (1982).

Yates, F.A., *Shakespeare's Last Plays: A New Approach* (Routledge & Kegan Paul, 1975).

Bacon

Dawkins, P., *Francis Bacon, Herald of a New Age* (Francis Bacon Research Trust l997).

Dawkins, P., *The Master (Part One)* (FBRT, 1993).

Dawkins, P., *Dedication to the Light,* (FBRT Journal, Series 1, Volume 3).

Henry, J., *Knowledge is Power, How Magic, the Government and an Apocalyptic Vision Inspired Francis Bacon to Create Modern Science* (Icon, 2002).

Lomas, R., *The Invisible College, The Royal Society, Freemasonry and the Birth of Modern Science* (Headline, 2002).

James I

Bevington & Holbrook (eds.) *The Politics of the Stuart Court Masque* (CUP, 1998).

Bingham, C., *James I of England* (Weidenfeld and Nicholson, 1981).

Fraser, A., *King James* (Weidenfeld and Nicholson, 1974).

McElwee, W., *The Wisest Fool in Christendom* (Faber, 1958).

Stewart, A., *The Cradle King, A Life of James VI and I* (Chatto and Windus, 2003).

Watson, G., *Bothwell and the Witches* (Robert Hale, 1975).

Williams, C., *James I* (Arthur Barker, 1934).

Other Books

Bald, R.C., *John Donne, A Life* (Clarendon Press, l970).

Barfield, O., *Romanticism Comes of Age* (Wesleyan, 1986).

Boardman, T., *Mapping the Millennium, Behind the Plans of the New World Order* (Temple Lodge, 1995).

Bock, E., *Kings and Prophets* (Floris, Edinburgh, 1989).

Brown Jnr. T., *Tom Brown's Field Guide to Nature Observation and Tracking* (Berkley, 1983).

Chambers, E., *Elizabethan Stage, Vol 2* (Clarendon Press, 1961).

Cooper-Oakley, I., *The Count of Saint Germain* (Garber, 1988).

Dawkins, P., *Building Paradise, The Freemasonic and Rosicrucian Six Days Work* (Francis Bacon Research Trust, 2001).

Day, C., *Consensus Design* (Architectural Press, 2003).

Edmunds, F., *The Quest for Meaning* (Continuum, New York, 1997).

Evans, J., *Rudolf II and his World, A Study in Intellectual History, 1576-1612* (OUP, 1973).

Gilbert, A., *The New Jerusalem* (Bantam, 2002).

Godwin, J., *Robert Fludd, Hermetic Philosopher and Surveyor of Two Worlds* (Thames and Hudson, 1979).

Hancox, J., *Kingdom for a Stage, Magicians and Aristocrats in Elizabethan Theatre* (Sutton, 2001).

Hancox, J., *The Byrom Collection* (Jonathan Cape, 1992).

Jonson, Ben, *The Complete Masques,* ed. Orgel, S. (Yale, 1986).

Kleeberg, L., *Wege und Worte, Erinnerungen an Rudolf Steiner* (Rudolf Gering, Basel, 1928).

McIntosh, C., *The Rosicrucians, The History, Mythology and Rituals of an Esoteric Order* (Samuel Weiser, 1998).

New English Bible (Oxford and Cambridge, 1970).

Prokoffief, S., *The Spiritual Origins of Eastern Europe and the Future Mysteries of the Holy Grail* (Temple Lodge, 1993).

Rygg, K., *Masqued Mysteries Unmasked* (Pendragon Press, 2000).

Sease, V. & Schmidt-Brabant, M., *Paths of the Christian Mysteries* (Temple Lodge, 2003).

Stein, W.J., *The Death of Merlin* (Floris, Edinburgh, 1989).

Steiner, R., *From Symptom to Reality in Modern History* (Rudolf Steiner Press, 1976).

Steiner, R., *Karmic Relationships Vol. 2* (Rudolf Steiner Press, 1997).

Steiner, R., *Lectures on the Gospel of St Mark* (Anthroposophic Press, 1986).

Steiner, R., *The Karma of Untruthfulness Vol. I* (Rudolf Steiner Press, 1988).

Steiner, R., *The Karma of Untruthfulness Vol. II* (Rudolf Steiner Press, 1992).

Steiner, R. (Bamford, C., ed.) *The Secret Stream, Christian Rosenkreutz and Rosicrucianism* (Anthroposophic Press, 2000).

Steiner, R., *The Temple Legend and the Golden Legend, Freemasonry and Related Occult Movements* (Rudolf Steiner Press, 1997).

Steiner, R., *Toward Imagination* (Anthroposophic Press, 1980).

Steiner, R. & Steiner-von Sivers, M., *Correspondence and Documents 1901–1925* (Rudolf Steiner Press, 1988).

Strong, R., *Britannia Triumphans* (Walter Neurath Memorial Lectures, 1980).

Wallace-Murphy & Hopkins, *Rosslyn* (Element Books, 1999).

Walton, I., *Life of Donne* (London, 1640).

Yates, F.A., *Giordano Bruno and the Hermetic Tradition* (University of Chicago Press, 1991).

Yates, F.A., *The Art of Memory* (Penguin, 1978).

Yates, F.A., *The Rosicrucian Enlightenment* (Routledge, 1972). (Includes Rosicrucian manifestos: *Fama Fraternitatis* and *Confessio Fraternitatis* as appendices.)

Yates, F.A., *Theatre of the World* (Routledge, 1987).

Yeats, W.B., *A Vision* (MacMillan Papermac, 1981).

ILLUSTRATION CREDITS

1. Panel painting of St. Mark the Evangelist, by Master Theodoric, Chapel of the Holy Cross, Karlstejn, Prague, 1360–1364.
2. James VI of Scotland in 1595, aged 29, by Adriaen Vanson. (By courtesy of Scottish Portrait Gallery.) Quotation from: *From Symptom to Reality in Modern History*, Rudolf Steiner, lecture 2, p. 46.
3. James I of England, 1621, by Daniel Mytens. (By courtesy of the National Portrait Gallery, London.) Quotation from: *From Symptom to Reality in Modern History*, Rudolf Steiner, lecture 2, p. 47.
4. Portrait of Francis Bacon—detail. (From: *The Advancement of Learning*.)
5. Detail from stained glass window with a portrait of King James, 1615. (By courtesy of the Trustees of the National Museums of Scotland.)
6. Bust of Shakespeare. (By courtesy of the Shakespeare Institute, University of Birmingham; © University of Birmingham.)
7. Jakob Boehme—sculpture in park at Zgorzelec (Goerlitz), Poland. Quotation from: *The Rosicrucian Foundations of the Age of Natural Science*, Ernst Lehrs, p.3.
8. Jakob Balde—detail. (From: *Carmina Lyrica*—1844.)
9. Jakob Boehme—detail. From frontispiece to *Theosophia Revelata*. (Courtesy of: Städtische Sammlungen für Geschichte und Kultur Goerlitz/Oberlausitzische Bibliothek der Wissenschaften.)
10. James I. Detail of image 3. (By courtesy of the National Portrait Gallery, London.)
11. Sir Francis Bacon, by Paul van Somer, c. 1618. Detail. (From the Gorhambury Collection. Photograph: Photographic Survey, Courtauld Institute of Art.)
12. William Shakespeare, attributed to John Taylor. Detail. (By

courtesy of the National Portrait Gallery, London. Quotation from: *The Birth of a New Agriculture*, ed. A. Graf v. Keyserlingk, Temple Lodge, London, 1999, p.59.

13. Frontispiece to Shakespeare's *First Folio*, 1623. William Blake spoke of this image to Crabb Robinson: 'I spoke again of the form of the persons who appear to him [Blake], and why he did not draw them. 'It is not worth while. There are so many. . . As to Shakespeare, he is exactly like the old engraving, which is called a bad one. I think it is very good.' *Diary, Reminiscences & Correspondence*, Henry Crabb Robinson, AMS Press, New York, 1967, Vol.2, p.15.

14. Frontispiece to Francis Bacon's *Of the Advancement and Proficiencie of Learning*, 1640. (Translated from Bacon's *De Dignitate et Augmentis Scientarium*, 1623.)

15, 16. Double frontispiece to King James's *Workes*, 1616.

17. Christmas Greeting to James 1 from Michael Maier (1612). Drawing by Adam McClean. (By courtesy of Adam McClean.)

18. From *Naometria* by Simon Studion (1604). (From microfilm of original in Warburg Institute, London.)

19. Psalm 46, King James Bible, (1611). (British Library Shelfmark: C35113(1)f.Ddd3r. By permission of the British Library.)

20. Shakespeare's Globe Education Brochure, 2003. (By courtesy of International Shakespeare Globe Centre.)